Grand Diplôme Cooking Course

Volume 7

Grand Diplôme Cooking Course

A Danbury Press Book

The Danbury Press

a division of Grolier Enterprises, Inc.

Robert B. Clarke   Publisher

This book has been adapted from the Grand Diplôme Cooking Course, originally published by Purnell Cookery, U.S.A.

Purnell Grand Diplôme Editorial Board

Rosemary Hume and Muriel Downes
Principals, London Cordon Bleu Cookery
School, England

Anne Willan	Editor
Eleanor Noderer	Associate Editor
Sheryl Julian	Assistant Editor
John Paton	Managing Editor
José Northey	Co-ordinating Editor
Peter Leather	Art Editor
Charles F. Turgeon	Wine Consultant

Library of Congress Catalog Card Number: 72-13896
© B.P.C. Publishing, 1971, and
© Phoebus Publishing, 1972.
Filmsetting by Petty and Sons Ltd., Leeds, England.
Printed in the United States of America

1234567899876543

All recipes have been tested either at the Cordon Bleu Cookery School in London or in our U.S. test kitchens.

Note: all recipe quantities in this book serve 4 people unless otherwise stated.

Contents

From the Editor

Dark, scented rye bread, touched with honey; chewy, hearty cracked wheat bread; nutty sourdough or crusty French bread — these and many other **Breads** become easy when you understand kneading and how yeast works. **Chocolate** holds a persistent power over many palates with scrumptious dishes like pears belle Hélène — poached pears coated with a rich orange chocolate sauce — and magali, melting little pastries filled with chocolate cream and topped with browned almonds. Baking bread and cooking with chocolate are just two of the skills you will master with the help of the methods of the London Cordon Bleu Cookery School in Volume 7 of your Grand Diplôme Cooking Course.

There's more advice on **Choosing and Carving Meat**, and this time lamb, pork and ham are spotlighted in charts showing the different cuts and how to cook them. For a change of pace, turn to economical **Vegetable Entrées**, or learn the secrets of **Preserving** familiar to our grandmothers for crystal-clear jellies, fruit-filled jams and rich relishes. Equally rooted in the past is **Russian Cooking**. Savor the peasant simplicity of Caucasian shashlik, designed by nomads to be cooked outdoors, then sample the sophistication of charlotte russe and other famous creations of the French chefs to the Tsarist Court.

For party givers, eyecatching canapés and cocktail hors d'oeuvre are explored in depth in one of four **Menus** that include recipes for coq au vin, braised stuffed leg of lamb, tipsy cake and Roquefort tartlets. You'll find other ideas for easy entertaining in **Cooking for a Cold Supper**, so send out the invitations. Bon Appétit!

Anne Willan

Coq au vin, a classic French dish, is surrounded with croûtes and sprinkled with parsley (recipe is on page 12)

THE CLASSIC COQ AU VIN

Begin this dinner menu with a simple soup or fill tartlets with Roquefort cheese for a touch of sophistication. Then serve coq au vin cooked in red Burgundy, followed by another French classic — refreshing cold lemon soufflé.

The rich, dark sauce that distinguishes this famous chicken dish suggests something fine to drink — from Burgundy's Côte de Beaune for instance. You may like to try one of the remarkably smooth, full-flavored wines from the town of Volnay. It is well worth the extra cost to buy one from one of the town's fine vineyards like Caillerets, Clos des Chênes or Clos des Ducs. A suitable alternative from our own country would be a Pinot Noir from the Santa Clara region of California.

Cream of Celery Soup
or
Roquefort Tartlets

Coq au Vin
Mashed Potatoes
Buttered Belgian Endive

Cold Lemon Soufflé

Red wine — Volnay (Côte de Beaune)
or Pinot Noir (California)

TIMETABLE

Day before
Prepare the soup but do not add the egg yolks or arrowroot liaison. Cover and refrigerate.
Cook coq au vin but do not thicken the sauce with kneaded butter. Cover securely and refrigerate.
Make pastry and filling for tartlets, store separately in refrigerator.

Morning
Make the soufflé but do not decorate; chill.
Line tartlet pans with dough, fill, add the lids and refrigerate.
Cut and fry the croûtes for the chicken.
Chop parsley for the chicken, and chop celery leaves for the soup; keep in a small bowl covered tightly with plastic wrap.

Prepare endive for cooking and keep in a plastic bag. Peel the potatoes and keep in cold water.

Assemble ingredients for final cooking from 6:45 for dinner around 8 p.m.

You will find that **cooking times** given in the individual recipes for these dishes have sometimes been adapted in the timetable to help you when cooking and serving this menu as a party meal.

Order of Work

6:45
Set oven at moderately hot (375°F) and arrange oven shelves so that chicken will be on the bottom *and cheese tartlets on the top.*
Trim wax paper or foil on soufflé dish and decorate the top of the soufflé.

7:10
Bake Roquefort tartlets.
Put cooked chicken in to heat. Boil potatoes.

7:30
Turn oven down to warm and let chicken *and tartlets* remain in oven to keep warm.
Warm croûtes.
Mash potatoes to a purée with seasoning and butter; cover with ½ cup of hot milk, cover and keep warm. Beat well just before serving.

7:45
Cook the endive.
Remove the wax paper or foil from soufflé and press the nuts around the sides.
Thicken sauce for chicken and add garnishes.
Reheat the soup and add the egg yolks or arrowroot.

8:00
Serve appetizer.

As an appetizer, serve homemade cream of celery soup

Appetizer

Cream of Celery Soup

bunch of celery, sliced
1 small onion, finely chopped
2½ cups chicken stock
salt and pepper
2 tablespoons butter
1 tablespoon flour
1½ cups milk
2 egg yolks, beaten to mix, or
   1 teaspoon arrowroot
4–5 tablespoons light cream
1 tablespoon chopped celery
   leaves (for garnish)–optional

Method
In a saucepan combine the celery, onion and stock and season to taste. Simmer gently for 20–30 minutes until the celery is soft, then work the mixture through a food mill or purée in a blender.

Melt the butter and stir in the flour off the heat. Add the celery purée, return to the heat and bring to a boil, stirring frequently. Simmer for several minutes, then add the milk, bring just to a boil, taste and correct the seasoning.

Mix the egg yolks or arrowroot with the cream until smooth. Remove the soup from the heat, stir about 2 tablespoons into the cream mixture and return this, stirring slowly, to the remaining soup. Reheat over low heat, stirring constantly, until the soup thickens.
Watchpoint: if using egg yolks, do not let the soup boil or it will curdle.

Sprinkle the soup with chopped celery leaves just before serving, if you like.

Alternative appetizer

Roquefort Tartlets

For rich pie pastry
$1\frac{1}{2}$ cups flour
pinch of salt
$\frac{1}{2}$ cup butter
1 egg yolk
1–2 tablespoons cold water

For filling
$\frac{3}{4}$ cup béchamel sauce, made with 1 tablespoon butter, 1 tablespoon flour, $\frac{3}{4}$ cup milk (infused with $\frac{1}{2}$ bay leaf, 6 peppercorns, blade of mace, slice of onion)
$\frac{1}{2}$ cup heavy cream
$\frac{1}{4}$ lb Roquefort cheese, mashed until smooth with a fork
3 egg yolks

8–9 tartlet pans or muffin tins; 2 fluted cookie cutters

Method
To make pastry dough: sift the flour with the salt into a bowl. Cut the butter into the flour until in small pieces and well coated. Then rub in with the fingertips until the mixture looks like crumbs. Make a well in the center, add the egg yolk and most of the water; stir to combine. Quickly draw the flour into the center of the mixture with a knife, adding more water if needed. Turn the dough onto a floured board or marble slab and knead. Wrap and chill 30 minutes.

To make the filling: make the béchamel sauce, then stir in the cream. While it is still warm, beat in the cheese and egg yolks; let cool. Set oven at moderately hot (375°F).

Roll out the pastry dough and, using a fluted cutter ($\frac{1}{2}$ inch larger than the pans), cut circles and line the pans. Cut smaller circles with a smaller cutter from the remaining dough to use as lids for the tartlets. Fill lined pans three-quarters full and set a lid on each one. Bake in heated oven for about 20 minutes or until pastry is golden brown. Serve the tartlets hot.

True Roquefort cheese comes from the place of the same name in the Aveyron district of France. It is made from curds of ewe's milk mixed with fine breadcrumbs that have been allowed to acquire a green mold. Experts consider Roquefort cheese at its best after a full year of ripening, although it is sold as mature after only 30–40 days storage in a cool but damp atmosphere (preferably one of the local natural caves). Cheese should have a yellowish tinge and be evenly veined in blue. Avoid chalky-looking Roquefort that isn't fully matured.

Fill tartlet cases three-quarters full before covering each one with a lid of dough and baking in oven

For an unusual appetizer, serve Roquefort tartlets

Entrée

Coq au Vin

3½—4 lb roasting chicken
¼ lb piece of bacon or salt pork
12 small onions
¼ cup butter
1 cup red Burgundy
2 cloves of garlic, crushed
bouquet garni
1—1½ cups chicken stock
salt and pepper
kneaded butter, made with
   2 tablespoons butter and
   1 tablespoon flour

For garnish
1 hard roll, sliced and fried in
   3—4 tablespoons oil and
   butter, mixed, for croûtes
1 tablespoon chopped parsley

Trussing needle and string

Method
Truss the chicken or tie it neatly; this is important even though the bird is cut into pieces later because it keeps it compact and makes it easy to turn while browning.

Cut the bacon or pork into lardons (¼ inch strips, 1—1½ inches long). To blanch the lardons and onions, cover them with cold water, bring to a boil and drain well.

Heat the butter in a flame-proof casserole, add the chicken and brown slowly on all sides. Remove from the casserole and add the bacon and onions. Brown these well and drain off excess fat. Cut the chicken into five serving pieces and return to the casserole.

Heat the wine in a separate pan, flame it and pour over the chicken while still flaming. (If the wine does not flame, boil to reduce it by about one-third and then add to the chicken.) Add the garlic,

bouquet garni and stock and season to taste. Cover and cook on top of the stove, over low heat, for 30—40 minutes or until the chicken is tender when tested with a fork. Alternatively bake in a moderately low oven (325°F) for 40—50 minutes.

Remove the chicken from the casserole and discard bouquet garni. Taste the sauce for seasoning and thicken it slightly by whisking in the kneaded butter a little at a time and cooking until thick.

Place the chicken pieces in a serving dish and pour over the sauce. Surround with croûtes and sprinkle with chopped parsley. Serve with mashed potatoes and buttered Belgian endive.

To make croûtes for coq au vin: fry the sliced roll, including the crust, in 3—4 tablespoons oil and butter, mixed, until golden brown. Drain croûtes well on paper towels. (Otherwise use triangles of bread with crusts removed.)

Dessert

Cold Lemon Soufflé

½ cup lemon juice
3 tablespoons finely grated
   lemon rind
4 eggs, separated
1 cup sugar
1½ envelopes gelatin
¼ cup cold water
1½ cups heavy cream, whipped
   until it holds a soft shape
¼ cup finely chopped pistachios
   or browned almonds

*Soufflé dish (1 quart capacity);
pastry bag and star tube*

Method
Wrap a strip of wax paper or foil around the soufflé dish so it comes 1½ inches above the dish; tie with string to make a collar. (This allows the cold soufflé to set above the top of the dish so it resembles a hot soufflé when the collar is removed.)

In a bowl combine the egg yolks, sugar, lemon juice and rind. Stand the bowl over a pan of hot water and beat until the sugar dissolves and is light and thickens enough to leave a trail for a few moments when the beater is lifted. Remove the bowl from the pan and continue beating until the mixture is cool. If using an electric beater, the pan of hot water is not necessary.

Sprinkle the gelatin over the cold water and let stand for about 5 minutes until spongy. Dissolve over a pan of hot water and stir into the lemon mixture. Beat the egg whites until they hold a soft shape.

Stand the soufflé mixture in a bowl of ice water and stir very gently until it starts to

thicken. With a metal spoon, carefully fold in the lightly whipped cream, followed by the egg whites. Pour at once into the prepared soufflé dish. The mixture should come 1—2 inches above the edge of the dish. Refrigerate 1—2 hours or until set. Not more than 1—2 hours before serving, trim the paper collar level with the soufflé mixture. Spread the top with the stiffly whipped cream, fill the rest into the pastry bag fitted with the star tube and decorate the edge of the soufflé with rosettes of cream. Just before serving, remove the paper collar and press pistachios or almonds around the exposed sides of the soufflé.

To brown whole almonds: blanch the almonds and remove the skins; bake the nuts for 8—10 minutes in a moderately hot oven (375°F) or until browned.

Beat the egg yolks, sugar, lemon rind and juice until the mixture is slightly thick

A classic entrée

Cold lemon soufflé is decorated with chopped pistachios and rosettes of whipped cream

Roast leg of lamb, with mint sauce served separately — see cooking and serving suggestions on page 17

HOW TO CHOOSE AND CARVE MEAT (2)

LAMB, PORK AND HAM

LAMB

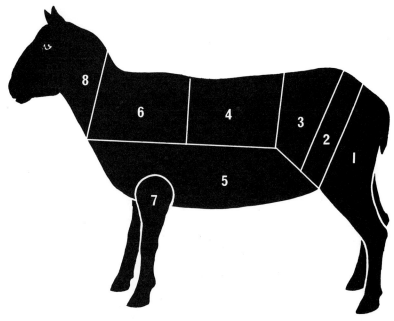

1	Leg	**5**	Breast
2	Sirloin	**6**	Shoulder
3	Loin	**7**	Foreshank
4	Rack	**8**	Neck

Choice of Cuts

Lamb varies greatly in size, depending on age. However, unless the animal is very small, lamb is divided into the same cuts, regardless of size.

Top quality young lamb has pink, fine-textured lean meat with firm fat – the color of the fat does not indicate quality as this varies with the age and breed. In older lambs, meat is light red and bones appear drier and harder.

Like beef, lamb is graded by the Department of Agriculture but its quality is generally more uniform.

Baby lamb, which is available in specialty markets in spring and early summer, is deliciously tender and succulent with enough natural fat for all cuts to be roasted. It tends to be in short supply and is expensive.

Lamb is easy to cook as it has plenty of natural fat and flavor and the meat is young so few cuts are tough. Here most people prefer to cook lamb until it is well done, but Europeans, particularly the French, insist that the flavor is more subtle when the meat is pink in the center.

The bones are best left in cuts of lamb as they add flavor and prevent shrinkage during cooking, although some roasts are boned and rolled for convenience in carving. Meat for stews or soup should have the bone included.

Carving Lamb

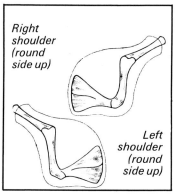

Right shoulder (round side up)

Left shoulder (round side up)

Shoulder and Leg

Carve both these cuts as shown in the photographs and captions on pages 18–19.

To carve a shoulder successfully, you need to know where the bones lie in relation to the meat, as this varies according to whether it is a left hand or right hand shoulder (see diagrams left). Before you start, decide from which side the shoulder is cut and set it on the board or platter so the meatiest part is on top.

Sirloin

Sometimes the sirloin is left as part of the leg of lamb, when it should be carved in diagonal slices, parallel to the backbone. It is also made into a separate cut, usually boned and rolled.

Saddle or Double Rack

Carve the slices parallel to the backbone.

Loin

Spear the loin firmly with a fork and examine the underneath to find the direction of the ribs. Lay the meat, ribs down, on a carving board and cut down between each rib to form chops.

Crown

Cut down between the rib bones to form chops.

Rack

Set the rack of ribs on a carving board or platter with the rib bones pointing up. Cut straight down between the bones to form chops, allowing 1–2 chops per person. Rack of lamb can also be made into the French cut called carré d'agneau (see photograph on page 19) or a crown roast – as with crown roast of pork (see photograph on page 22).

To roast a carré d'agneau, allow 18 minutes per lb plus 18 minutes more (160°F on meat thermometer) for rare meat or 20 minutes per lb plus 20 minutes more for well done meat (175°F on meat thermometer). Carve by slicing down between each bone.

CUT OF LAMB	HOW TO COOK	COOKING AND SERVING SUGGESTIONS
1 Leg	Roast, pot roast or braise	Roast with parsley and breadcrumb coating, serve with wine gravy or mint sauce; pot roast with red wine and onions; braise with red wine and tomatoes
Hind shank	Simmer, braise or stew	Simmer for soup; braise or stew as goulash or Navarin
2 Sirloin roast	Roast or pot roast	Roast and pot roast as for leg
Sirloin chop	Broil, pan fry or stew	Broil or pan fry and serve with ratatouille and pilaf; stew with onions and tomatoes
3 Loin roast	Roast, pot roast or braise	Roast and stuff à la bretonne or portugaise; pot roast with onions, red or green peppers, tomatoes and eggplant; braise à l'Orloff
Loin chop or English chop (double loin with kidney)	Broil or pan fry	Serve with soubise or chasseur sauce
4 Rack or rib roast	Roast or broil	Serve with green beans and Anna or boulangère potatoes
Saddle or double rack	Roast	Serve as for rack
Crown roast	Roast	Stuff with rice, herbs and nuts; serve with wine gravy and artichoke hearts
Rib chop	Broil or pan fry	Serve with straw potatoes and glazed onions
5 Breast	Roast, pot roast or braise	Stuff with rice, herbs and nuts; serve with white wine gravy
Riblets	Barbecue, broil or stew	Barbecue or broil with spiced marinade; stew with root vegetables
6 Shoulder	Roast or pot roast	Stuff with cooked rice or kasha; serve with baked tomatoes and stuffed prunes; roast and stuff with chicken livers and raisins
Arm chop, blade chop, Saratoga chop	Broil, pan fry or stew	Broil and serve with fried apple rings and dauphinois potatoes; stuff with apple and pan fry; serve with white wine gravy; stew as Navarin or cassoulet
7 Foreshank	Simmer, braise or stew	Cook as for hind shank
8 Neck	Simmer or stew	Simmer for Scotch broth; Irish stew
Kidneys	Broil, pan fry or braise	Broil or pan fry and serve with mushrooms, tomatoes and dauphinois potatoes; braise with red wine, onions and mushrooms or port and sour cream
Tongue	Simmer, then chill or braise	Serve cold with Cumberland or Gribiche sauce; braise with white wine and grapes, or sherry and spinach
Heart	Braise	Stuff with herbs
Sweetbreads	Blanch, then braise or fry	Braise and serve with white wine sauce, onions, mushrooms and ham; fry and serve with tartare sauce
Brains	Blanch, then simmer	Serve with black butter or in red wine sauce with onions, bacon and mushrooms

Carving a Shoulder

1 Set shoulder on a carving platter with the meatiest side up and the knuckle away from you (this may be to the right or to the left, see diagrams on page 16). Tilt the meat slightly towards you and cut down to the bone in wedge-shaped slices

2 With a fork, find spine of the blade bone (the ridge along the top of the bone); cut wedge-shaped slices length-wise on either side of bone

3 Turn meat over and carve thin diagonal slices from the flat part of the blade bone

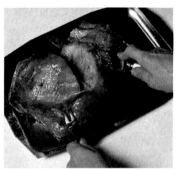

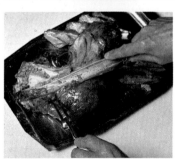

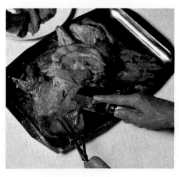

Carving a Saddle

1 Set saddle on a carving platter with the tail end towards you. Run the knife down one side of the back-bone and cut under the meat that lies on the side of it

2 Repeat this on other side of the bone. Carve 2–3 wedge-shaped slices down the whole length of each side of the back-bone, cutting the pieces in half if the saddle is large

3 Cut slanting slices from tail end of the saddle as shown below and, for those who like a little fat, cut slanting slices from the crisp flap of the neck

Carving a Leg

1 Set leg on a carving platter with the round side up and the knuckle nearest to you. Insert the fork near the knuckle and make the first cut diagonally down to the bone. Then make another cut $\frac{1}{4}$–$\frac{1}{2}$ inch towards the right to give a wedge-shaped slice; this part has the sweetest meat

2 Continue to carve in this way, working towards pelvic bone and slanting the knife more with each slice. When you reach this bone, turn the leg over and carve thin slices sideways and parallel to the leg bone

To Prepare Carré d'Agneau

1 For a carré d'agneau, use a 2 lb rack of lamb. Remove the chine bone (the part of the backbone that joins the ribs together), if not already done, and saw a line across the rib bones about 3 inches from the meat.

2 Place the rack upright and, with a sharp knife, working from the saw line, cut out and then remove the short ends of the rib bones.

3 Cut underneath and loosen the remaining rib bones to within $\frac{1}{2}$ inch of the meat, but leave the bones attached. If the meat is very fat, trim away a layer of fat.

4 Make slits through the meat about $1\frac{1}{2}$ inches long, by running the blade of the knife along the side of each rib bone, starting from the sawn edge of the bones. Then push the bones through the slits.

5 Draw the flap up and back towards the lean meat and pull it over so the edges of the fat join and completely en-circle the lean. Trim off any of the fat flap that overlaps.

6 Tie up the meat: bring the string around it in the slits between each rib bone.

Cooked rack of lamb is tied in French style (carré d'agneau) and garnished with chop frills

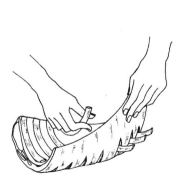

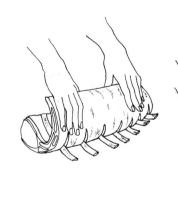

PORK

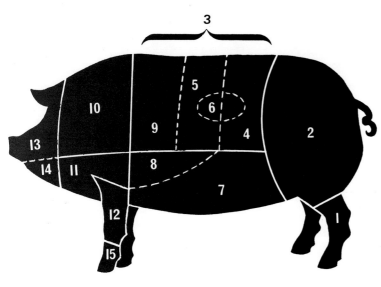

1	Hind foot	6	Tenderloin	11	Picnic shoulder
2	Fresh ham	7	Flank	12	Hock
3	Fat back	8	Spareribs	13	Snout
4	Sirloin	9	Blade loin	14	Jowl
5	Loin	10	Boston butt	15	Fore foot

Choice of Cuts

The meat of the pig is invaluable to the cook — it provides ham, bacon and salt pork as well as delicious fresh cuts like loin and spareribs. Like most animals, the best and therefore the most expensive cuts of the pig are towards the hindquarters, near the hams. The variety meats are less delicate than in other animals, but they are often used in sausages. The pig, in one form or another, is edible from its snout to the tip of its curly tail.

Good pork is pinkish grey with firm white fat. Like lamb, pork is best when young and, in general, the older the animal, the darker the color, although some breeds naturally yield a darker lean meat. Cured pork should be a good healthy shade of pink, darkening to deep red, depending on the cure.

Pork is a rich meat, full of natural fat, which is why it is so good for curing as ham and bacon. Do not cut off all fat from fresh pork because fat gives a great deal of flavor to lean meat.

All fresh pork and pork products like sausages must be cooked until they are well done with no trace of pink juice. Long cooking also helps to melt the pork fat so it is important to drain or skim pork dishes thoroughly to remove the fat.

Loin is the favorite cut of pork for roasting but fresh ham (leg) is also delicious roasted when available. Pot roasting and braising are good methods of cooking most other pork roasts because, despite its richness, pork can dry out during long cooking when oven roasted unless it is basted often. Similarly, pork chops are best when pan fried or cooked with a little liquid as they tend to be dry when broiled unless they are very thickly cut.

In any pork dish, spices like cloves and tart flavors such as apple, pineapple and wine help to counteract the richness.

Carving Pork

Loin

For center cut loin: spear the loin firmly with a fork and examine the underneath to find the direction of the ribs. Lay the meat, ribs down, on a carving board and cut down between each rib to form chops. The blade end of the loin contains some of the shoulder bone as well: cut away the rib chops (as for the loin) as far as the shoulder bone, then carve horizontal slices from above and around the bone.

Sirloin Roast

It is much easier to buy a sirloin roast boned and rolled because, although one end of the roast can be cut into chops like the loin, the other end contains the hip and slices must be cut around it.

Tenderloin

Carve this boneless cut in thin diagonal slices.

Boston Butt and Picnic Shoulder

Boston butt is the upper half of the pork shoulder and the picnic shoulder is the lower half. Like the sirloin roast, they are often boned and rolled or stuffed cushion fashion. If they have the bone in, look at the diagrams and follow the same instructions as for carving shoulder of lamb (see pages 18–19).

Fresh Ham or Leg of Pork

Carve as for ham and cured pork (see page 24).

REGULAR ROASTING TIMES		
TOTAL COOKING TIME (at 375°F Oven Temperature)		**On Meat Thermometer**
Lamb Medium: 18 minutes per lb plus 18 minutes more		160°F
Well done: 20 minutes per lb plus 20 minutes more		175°F
Pork 25 minutes per lb plus 25 minutes more		185°F

CUT OF PORK	HOW TO COOK	COOKING AND SERVING SUGGESTIONS
1 Hind foot	Boil, then braise or broil	Boil for soup and aspic; boil then braise for bœuf à la mode en gelée or with onions; boil, then broil with breadcrumbs and brush with devil sauce
2 Fresh ham (leg), whole, shank half, butt half	Roast or pot roast	Serve with spiced apples, roast potatoes or braised chestnuts and wine gravy
Slice or pork steak	Pan fry or braise	Pan fry with tomatoes; stuff with herb or apple mixture and braise in white wine
3 Fat back	Pan fry	Use for salt pork or lard
4 Sirloin roast	Roast, pot roast or braise	Roast as for loin roast; pot roast with white wine and serve with pilaf and stuffed prunes; braise with celery and onions
Sirloin chop	Pan fry or stew	Pan fry with onions and apple rings; stew with onion, green pepper and tomato
5 Loin roast	Roast or pot roast	Roast and serve with glazed onions and carrots Vichy; pot roast with onions and tomatoes
Crown roast	Roast	Fill center with herb or chestnut stuffing and serve as for loin roast
Loin chops	Pan fry or stew	Serve as for sirloin chop; serve with dijonnaise sauce and sautéed potatoes
6 Tenderloin	Pot roast or braise	Serve with mushrooms and sour cream sauce or with cider sauce and apples; stuff with prunes
7 Flank	Pan fry	Use for salt pork or bacon
8 Spareribs	Roast or broil	Baste with sweet and sour marinade
9 Blade loin	Pot roast or braise	Serve as for sirloin roast
10 Boston butt	Pot roast or braise	Pot roast with spices and stock; braise with onions, green pepper and tomatoes or with sauerkraut, ham and sausages
11 Picnic shoulder	Pot roast or braise	Serve as for Boston butt
Arm steak	Stew	Stew with onions and peppers
12 Hock	Braise or simmer	Braise with sauerkraut and sausages; simmer and serve with cranberry or mustard sauce
13 Snout	Simmer	Simmer with seasonings and garlic and serve hot with Tabasco sauce
14 Jowl	Pan fry	Use for bacon
15 Fore foot	Boil, then braise or broil	Serve as for hind foot

To Prepare
Crown Pork Roast

You will need 2 pork loins, each weighing about 4 lb. The chine bone (part of the backbone) should be removed so that the ribs are no longer attached to each other.

With a sharp knife, cut through the flesh about 1 inch from the end of the rib bones. Do the same for the second pork loin

Remove the fat and meat from the ends of the bones and scrape them clean

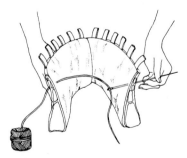

With fine string and a trussing needle, sew the pieces of meat together, back to back (i.e. fat inside) with the bones curving out

HAM AND CURED PORK

Ham, the hind leg of pork, is cured by salting and soaking in brine, by smoking, or by a combination of both.

Cures vary from mild to sweet to piquant and the cure determines the method of preparation.

Several other cuts are cured like ham, although none of them compare in flavor and tenderness to ham itself.

Types of Ham

Country hams are sold cured in a variety of ways; they are uncooked and may need soaking to remove excess salt before they are boiled.

A well-aged **country ham** such as a Virginia ham, that is cured with a good deal of salt, must be soaked for 12–24 hours, then simmered in water before it is baked. You can tell from the dry hard surface of the meat when a great deal of salt has been used in curing, but if in doubt, ask advice in the market where you are buying it.

Many southern states, among them Tennessee, Georgia and Kentucky, claim to produce the best ham, but Smithfield, Virginia hams have for many years been reputed to be the best. Settlers in Virginia began exporting bacon and pork to New England as long ago as 1639.

Regular hams, sometimes called 'cook-before-eating' or 'pre-cooked' or 'processed' hams, are mildly cured and come partially cooked. They must be simmered and baked

again before eating, but for a much shorter time than country hams. They need no soaking.

Completely cooked ham is sold whole or sliced for sandwiches, cold meat dishes, etc.

Other Cuts

Canadian bacon, made from the meat that runs along the loin of fresh pork, is almost solid lean meat, and is a good choice for a small family. However, it can dry out if it is not cooked carefully.

Boned shoulder butt resembles Canadian bacon but it contains more fat.

Smoked picnic shoulder is a large cut that is cured like ham and can be cooked in the same way; it contains a good deal more bone and fat and the meat is coarser.

Whole hams vary in size from 10–18 lb, depending on the size of the pig, and $\frac{1}{2}-\frac{3}{4}$ lb meat from a hot or cold ham, bone in, will serve one person. For boneless ham, allow 6–8 oz per person, depending on how much fat is included in the cut.

HAM AND CURED PORK

CUT OF HAM AND CURED PORK	HOW TO COOK	COOKING AND SERVING SUGGESTIONS
2 Ham, whole, butt half	Simmer or roast	Simmer and serve with spinach and Madeira sauce; roast with pineapple and sugar glaze and serve hot with sweet potatoes or cold with Cumberland sauce
Shank half	Simmer and braise	Serve with cream sauce or Véronique garnish
Ham slice	Roast, braise or pan fry	Roast as for ham; braise as for shank; pan fry with apple and orange slices
5 Canadian bacon, whole	Roast or braise	Roast as for ham; braise as for shank half
Canadian bacon, sliced	Pan fry	Serve with Madeira sauce
10 Smoked shoulder butt	Simmer	Simmer with carrots and onions and serve with parsley sauce
11 Smoked picnic shoulder	Simmer	Serve with sauerkraut or with boiled potatoes and spicy mustard sauce
12 Smoked hock	Simmer or braise	Serve as for smoked shoulder butt

Carving Ham and Cured Pork

Set the ham on a carving board with the shank bone towards you, rounded side of the ham away from you. With a long thin knife, make a cut about 3 inches from the shank bone, first inserting a fork right down to the board on the side of the bone nearest you.

Slice the ham in wedge-shaped slices a little less than $\frac{1}{4}$ inch thick, taking the knife right down to the bone and removing the slices as you go. Continue to slice thinly down to the bone and, after the first 12 slices or so, begin to slant the knife so that when the top bone is reached, the knife is almost flat as you carve.

To keep the ham neat, make sure that the knife goes right down to the bone with each slice and, from time to time, trim off small pieces that lie on the other side of the bone.

The ham slices may be arranged, overlapping, on a platter or they may be placed back on the ham so it is re-shaped for serving.

To carve a ham by the method used in restaurants and delicatessens, you need a ham stand and a ham knife. Slice the ham lengthwise, cutting with the grain instead of across, as in the first method. Start carving on the rounded side, and allow the knife to travel from the top bone down to the shank, cutting very thin slices.

Ham Shank
Set the ham on a carving board with the shank pointing to the left. Cut the ham in half lengthwise, parallel to the shank bone. Set the boneless piece of ham, cut side down, on the board and carve it into vertical slices across the grain of the meat. Turn over remaining half of ham, so the bone is down; carve vertical slices down to bone.

Shoulder
Carve as for shoulder of lamb.

Ham Butt
Set the ham, cut side down, on a carving board. Cut it in half vertically, working parallel to the shank bone. Set boneless piece of ham, cut side down, on the carving board and carve into vertical slices. Leave the remaining piece of ham with the shank bone pointing down. Carve horizontal slices from each side of this bone.

Canadian Bacon and Shoulder Butt
Cut straight down across the grain in three-eighth inch thick slices.

Maple baked ham may be served hot or cold with raisin sauce

COOKING WITH PORK AND HAM

To Cook a Country Ham

If the ham has been strongly cured, soak it for 12–24 hours in water to cover, changing the water once or twice.

To cook: drain and place the ham in a large kettle with water to cover, 1 onion stuck with 6 cloves, 8–12 peppercorns, 2 bay leaves and 6 whole allspice berries. If you like, substitute cider for $\frac{1}{4}$ of the amount of water for cooking and add 2 halved apples to the liquid, with the other seasonings. Cover kettle,

bring to a boil and simmer very gently (see the cooking times chart, below).

If serving cold, cool the ham in the water until tepid, take it out, discarding the cooking liquid, and carefully peel off the skin. (If it peels off easily, the ham is thoroughly cooked.) Coat the ham with browned crumbs, pressing them on to form a covering. Alternatively, simmer ham, cool and skin, then coat and bake as for any regular ham.

If serving hot, take the ham from the cooking liquid and peel it while still hot.

COOKING TIMES FOR COUNTRY HAMS

CUT	WEIGHT	TIME
Small pieces of ham	$1\frac{1}{2}$–2 lb 3 lb and over	1–$1\frac{1}{2}$ hours 30 minutes per lb
Whole hams		Allow 20 minutes per lb plus 20 minutes more

Maple Baked Ham

2–$2\frac{1}{2}$ lb ham butt or $2\frac{1}{2}$–3 lb ham shank

For simmering (optional)
1 onion, stuck with a clove
6 peppercorns
1 bay leaf

For baking
1 cup maple syrup
$\frac{1}{2}$ teaspoon ground ginger
$\frac{1}{4}$ teaspoon ground nutmeg
$\frac{1}{4}$ teaspoon ground allspice
12–16 whole cloves

Method

If using a country ham, soak it for 6–8 hours if it is salty, then drain it.

In a kettle cover the ham with cold water, bring it slowly to a boil and skim well. Add the onion, peppercorns and bay leaf, cover and simmer 1–$1\frac{1}{2}$ hours. Let cool in the liquid, drain it and remove the skin. Regular hams need no simmering.

Score the fat of the ham in diamonds and stud each one with a clove. Mix the maple syrup with the ground spices.

Set the ham in a roasting pan, pour over the maple mixture and bake in a moderate oven (350°F), basting often, for $\frac{3}{4}$–1 hour or until the ham is well glazed and shiny. Serve hot or cold with raisin sauce.

Raisin Sauce

$\frac{1}{2}$ cup raisins, cut or chopped into small pieces
1 cup sugar
$\frac{1}{2}$ cup water
1 tablespoon Worcestershire sauce
2 tablespoons butter
3 tablespoons wine vinegar
few drops of Tabasco
salt and pepper
pinch of ground mace
$\frac{1}{4}$ cup red currant jelly

Method

Dissolve the sugar in the water, then boil steadily for 5 minutes. Add the remaining ingredients and simmer gently until the red currant jelly has dissolved. Serve hot or cold.

Barbecued Spareribs

4 lb spareribs, cut in 1–2 rib pieces
3 tablespoons soy sauce
$1\frac{1}{2}$ tablespoons sugar
$\frac{1}{4}$ cup tomato ketchup
3 tablespoons honey
$1\frac{1}{2}$ cups chicken stock

Method

Thoroughly mix the soy sauce, sugar, ketchup, honey and 1 cup stock together and marinate the spareribs in this mixture for 1 hour. Set oven at moderate (350°F).

Lift the spareribs from the marinade and lay on a rack in a roasting pan containing a little water to prevent smoking. Roast in heated oven for about $1\frac{1}{2}$ hours, turning the ribs from time to time, until they are brown and tender. Transfer to a platter.

Dilute the marinade with remaining stock, bring to a boil and pour over the spareribs to serve.

Serve spicy barbecued spareribs in a piquant sauce, made from their marinade (recipe is on page 25)

Bacon Pâté

1 lb sliced bacon
1 lb ground pork
1 small onion, finely chopped
2 cups fresh white breadcrumbs
2 hard-cooked eggs, chopped
pinch of ground mace
2 eggs, beaten to mix
salt and pepper

Large loaf pan (9 X 5 X 3 inches)

Method
Line the loaf pan with 4–5 slices of the bacon; reserve 6–8 slices and grind or finely chop the rest. Mix this with the pork, onion, breadcrumbs, hard-cooked eggs and mace. Stir in the beaten eggs to bind the mixture and season. When thoroughly mixed, press a layer into the loaf pan and smooth the top. Cover with 3–4 slices of reserved bacon, then press in another layer of the meat mixture. Cover with the remaining bacon and fill up with the meat mixture. Smooth the top and cover with foil.

Set the pan in a water bath and bake in a moderately low oven (325°F) for 1¼–1½ hours or until the pâté is firm and a skewer inserted in the center for 1 minute is hot to the touch when withdrawn. Take from the oven, top with a small plate and a light weight (about 2 lb) and cool.

To serve, turn out and cut into slices. This pâté will keep 1–2 days in the refrigerator.

Pork Chops Dijonnaise

4 thickly cut or butterfly pork chops or 8 thin pork chops
2 tablespoons butter
1 tablespoon oil
6 tablespoons grated Parmesan cheese
6 tablespoons heavy cream
6 tablespoons cider
2 teaspoons white wine vinegar
1 cup stock
1½ teaspoons Dijon-style mustard
salt and pepper

Method
In a skillet or shallow flame-proof casserole heat the butter and oil and brown the chops lightly on both sides.

Mix the cheese to a paste with 1–2 tablespoons cream and spread over the top of the chops. Bake in a moderately hot oven (375°F) for 25–40 minutes or until they are tender, depending on the thickness of the chops. Transfer the chops to a platter and keep warm.

Add the cider and vinegar to the pan and boil until reduced to a glaze. Add the stock, remaining cream, mustard and seasoning to taste. Reheat the sauce without boiling and spoon it over the chops.

Serve with sautéed potatoes and braised green cabbage.

Braised Green Cabbage

1 firm head of green cabbage, shredded
2 tablespoons butter
1 large onion, sliced
1 tart apple, pared, cored and sliced
salt and pepper
1–2 tablespoons stock

Method
Heat the butter in a flame-proof casserole and cook the onion until soft but not brown. Add the cabbage with the apple and seasoning, stir well and pour in the stock.

Cover with foil and a lid and braise in a moderately low oven (325°F) for 45 minutes or until the cabbage is very tender.

Lentil Purée

Soak 1 cup lentils overnight and drain. Combine them in a saucepan with an onion stuck with 1 clove, 1 carrot cut in rounds, a bouquet garni, little salt and plenty of water. Simmer 1–1½ hours or until tender.

Remove the bouquet garni and clove; work the mixture through a sieve or purée in a blender. Reheat; if too thick, thin with a little stock. Take from heat and beat in ¼ cup butter with pepper to taste. Stir in 1 stalk of very finely chopped celery.

Pork Tenderloins with Cider

2–3 (about 1½ lb) pork tenderloins
2 tablespoons oil
1 tablespoon butter
1 onion, finely chopped
1 dessert apple, quartered, cored and sliced
¾ cup cider
¾ cup stock
salt and pepper
kneaded butter, made with 2 tablespoons butter and 1 tablespoon flour
1 tablespoon chopped parsley

For garnish
2–3 apples, pared, cored and sliced
¼ cup butter

Method
In a skillet heat the oil and butter and brown the tenderloins all over. Take out and add the onion and apple. Fry for a few minutes until soft, then put back the meat with the cider and stock. Season, cover and simmer 25–30 minutes or until tender. Take out the tenderloins, cut into thin diagonal slices and keep warm.

Strain the cooking liquid, bring to a boil and thicken lightly by beating in the kneaded butter a little at a time. Adjust the seasoning, add parsley and put back the pork. Keep warm.

To prepare the garnish: heat the butter and fry the apple slices quickly until browned on both sides.

Arrange the tenderloins on a platter, spoon over the sauce, add the apple garnish, and serve with lentil purée.

Braised ham with Burgundy is garnished with watercress

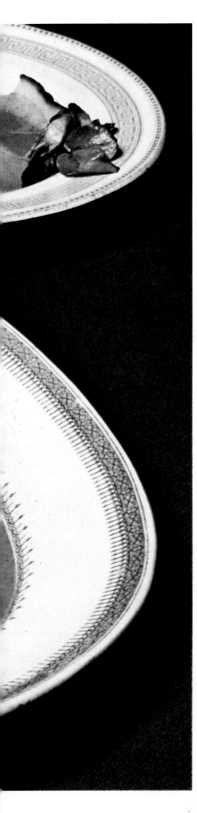

Jambon Bourguignonne
(Braised Ham with Burgundy)

2–2½ lb ham butt or 2½–3 lb
   ham shank
½ cup heavy cream
kneaded butter, made with 1½
   tablespoons butter and
   ¾ tablespoon flour
bunch of watercress (for
   garnish)

For braising
2 tablespoons butter
2 onions, sliced
2 carrots, sliced
1 stalk of celery, sliced
1½ cups red Burgundy wine
bouquet garni
salt and pepper

Method
If using a country ham, soak
in cold water for 6–8 hours
if it is salty, then drain it.

In a kettle cover the ham
with cold water, cover the
pan and simmer 1 hour. Let
cool in the liquid, drain
and dry with paper towels.
Regular ham needs no sim-
mering.

For braising: in a large
flameproof casserole melt
the butter and brown the ham
on all sides. Take out, add the
vegetables and cook gently,
covered, for 5–7 minutes
until the butter is absorbed.
Replace the ham, pour over the
wine and add the bouquet
garni and seasoning. Cover
and braise in a moderately low
oven (325°F) for 1½ hours or
until the ham is very tender.
Transfer the ham to a platter
and keep warm.

Strain the cooking liquid
and skim off all the fat. Bring
the liquid to a boil and whisk
in the kneaded butter, piece
by piece, cooking until the
sauce thickens. Add the
cream, bring just back to a boil

and taste for seasoning.

Carve a few slices from
the ham, spoon a little sauce
over them and serve the rest
separately. Garnish the platter
with watercress and serve
mashed potatoes separately.

Kneaded Butter
(Beurre Manié)

This is a liaison of twice
as much butter as flour
worked together as a
paste on a plate with a
fork. It is added in small
pieces to thicken a
mixture or liquid (usually
at the end of cooking).

Ham à la Crème

2–2½ lb ham butt or 2½–3 lb
   ham shank
1 onion, stuck with 1 clove
6 peppercorns
1 bay leaf
1 tablespoon butter (to finish)

For sauce
2 tablespoons butter
2 tablespoons flour
½ cup veal stock
1½ cups milk
salt
black pepper, freshly ground
½ cup light cream
3 tablespoons grated Gruyère
   or Parmesan cheese

Method
Soak country ham 6–8 hours
if necessary. In a kettle cover
the ham with cold water, bring
slowly to a boil and then skim
well. Add the onion, peppercorns and bay leaf, cover and
bring to a boil. Simmer gently
for 1½–2 hours for a country
ham, or 1 hour for a regular
ham. Cool in the liquid for 15
minutes.

To make the sauce: melt the
butter, stir in the flour and pour
on the stock and milk. Bring to
a boil, stirring, season and
simmer gently for 15 minutes
or until the sauce is creamy.
Stir in the cream, take from
heat, add the cheese and taste
the sauce for seasoning.

Pour a little of the sauce
into a shallow baking dish.
Drain the ham, remove any
skin and carve ham into even
slices. Arrange these on the
sauce, spoon remaining sauce
on top and dot with 1 tablespoon butter. Brown the ham
in a hot oven (400°F) for 5–
10 minutes or under the
broiler.

Ham Véronique

1½–2 lb Canadian bacon
1 onion, halved
1 stalk of celery, halved
1 carrot, sliced
bouquet garni
squeeze of lemon juice
½ lb seedless green grapes
¼ cup heavy cream

For butter sauce
½ cup white wine
2 teaspoons finely chopped
  onion
2 egg yolks
6 tablespoons butter

For velouté sauce
2 tablespoons butter
1½ tablespoons flour
1½–2 cups veal stock

Method
Remove any protective covering from the bacon. Put the meat in a kettle with the onion, celery, carrot, bouquet garni and water to cover, add the lid, bring to a boil and simmer gently for 40 minutes.

Add a squeeze of lemon juice to the grapes and keep covered in a bowl.

To make the butter sauce: boil the wine with the onion to reduce it by about one-third. Beat the egg yolks until slightly thick, strain on the wine and add 1 teaspoon butter. Stir the mixture in a water bath or in a double boiler over hot but not boiling water until thick. Add the remaining butter, a little at a time, and cook until the sauce has the consistency of thick cream.
Watchpoint: do not let it boil or it will curdle.

To make the velouté sauce: melt the butter, stir in the flour, cook until straw-colored and pour on the stock. Bring to a boil, stirring, and simmer 2–3 minutes. Take from the heat, beat in the butter sauce

a little at a time and add the cream. Reheat the sauce carefully without boiling. Add the grapes, taste for seasoning and keep warm.

Drain the bacon, slice it and arrange on a platter. Coat with a little of the sauce and serve the rest separately. Serve with small new or château potatoes (see recipe on page 109).

Sweet and Sour Mustard Sauce

2 cups brown sugar
½ cup dry mustard
1½ tablespoons arrowroot
pinch of salt
1 cup beef stock
1 cup vinegar
4 eggs, beaten to mix

Makes about 4 cups (to serve 12–15 people).

Method
Mix together the sugar, mustard, arrowroot and salt. Stir in the beef stock with the vinegar. Add the beaten eggs, mix well and cook the mixture over low heat, stirring constantly, until it thickens. Do not let it boil. Cool.

Graham Cracker Crusted Ham

10–12 lb regular ham
¼ cup honey
1 tablespoon grated onion
¾ cup graham cracker crumbs
1 teaspoon dry mustard
1 teaspoon ground ginger
½ teaspoon grated lemon rind
whole cloves

Serves 12–15 people.

Method
Place the ham, fat side up, on a rack in a roasting pan. Bake in a moderate oven (350°F), allowing 10 minutes per lb. Three-quarters of an hour before the end of cooking, remove any remaining skin. When cooked, score the fat

30

deeply in a diamond pattern.

Melt the honey, add the grated onion and brush this mixture on the ham. Mix the graham cracker crumbs, mustard, ginger and lemon rind and spread on the ham, pressing it firmly to form a coating. Stud the coating with cloves. Return to the oven and bake 45 minutes longer or until a meat thermometer registers 160°F. Cool. Serve with sweet and sour mustard sauce.

Braised Ham with Madeira Sauce

2–2½ lb butt or 2½–3 lb shank, of ham
creamed spinach (to serve)

For braising
2 tablespoons butter
2 onions, sliced
2 carrots, sliced
1 small turnip, sliced (optional)
1 stalk of celery, sliced
¼ cup Madeira or sherry (optional)
¾ cup well-flavored brown stock
bouquet garni
salt and pepper

For Madeira sauce
2 tablespoons oil
1½ tablespoons flour
3 cups well-flavored brown stock
½ teaspoon tomato paste
¼ cup Madeira or sherry

Tammy strainer

Method
To prepare a country ham: if necessary, soak the ham in cold water for 12 hours and drain. Put it in a kettle with water to cover, cover the pan, simmer 1 hour and drain. A regular ham needs no simmering.

For braising: in a large flameproof casserole melt the butter and cook the vegetables, covered, over gentle heat for 5–7 minutes. Place ham on top, pour over the Madeira or sherry, if used, and flame to burn off the alcohol. Add the stock, bouquet garni and seasoning. Cover with foil and the lid and braise in a moderately low oven (325°F) for 1½ hours or until the ham is very tender.

To make the Madeira sauce: heat the oil, stir in the flour and cook until straw-colored. Stir in the stock and tomato paste, bring to a boil and simmer, uncovered, for about 45 minutes, skimming frequently. When well reduced and clear, strain the sauce through a tammy strainer. Boil Madeira or sherry until reduced by half and add to the sauce. If the 'fonds' or juices from braising are not too fat or salty, these may be strained, reduced and added to the sauce.

Spoon the creamed spinach down the center of a platter, remove any skin from the ham and cut the ham in thin slices, arranging them on top of the creamed spinach. Serve with mashed potatoes or with small new potatoes tossed in butter and chopped parsley.

A tammy strainer is made of very fine double-mesh wire. When a sauce is worked through a tammy strainer it emulsifies and becomes smooth and glossy. A **tammy cloth** of rough-textured material like coarse flannel can be used instead, but this is less common. If no tammy strainer is available, use a fine regular strainer.

Creamed Spinach

1½ lb spinach
1 tablespoon butter
1–2 tablespoons heavy cream
salt and pepper (to taste)
pinch of nutmeg

Method
Wash spinach thoroughly, discard the tough stems and cook in boiling salted water for 5 minutes or until just tender. Drain and press it well with a spoon or plate to remove as much water as possible. Work through a sieve or purée in a blender.

Melt the butter in a pan, add the spinach and cook for a few minutes until dry. Then add heavy cream and heat well. Season with salt, pepper and nutmeg.

Cold Ham Mousse

1½ cups chopped cooked ham
1 cup chopped celery
1 envelope gelatin
¾ cup stock or white wine
½ green pepper, cored, seeded, diced and blanched
salt and pepper
¾ cup heavy cream, whipped until it holds a soft shape
bunch of watercress (for garnish)

Ring mold (1½ quart capacity)

Method
Sprinkle the gelatin over half the stock or wine in a small pan and let stand 5 minutes or until spongy. Dissolve over gentle heat, stir in the remaining liquid and stir into the ham and celery. Add blanched pepper and season well. Fold in the whipped cream and spoon the mixture into the ring mold. Cover and chill 2 hours or until set.

Just before serving unmold the mousse by lowering it into a pan of hand-hot water so the water just reaches the top edge of the mold and hold a few seconds. Then ease the mousse gently sideways with fingers to loosen it. Put the platter over the mold and quickly turn both over together, holding firmly. Give a sharp shake sideways to unmold.

Garnish the center with watercress and serve with orange and onion salad.

Orange and Onion Salad

4 navel oranges, peeled and sliced
2 mild or Bermuda onions
¼ cup vinaigrette dressing

Method
Slice the onion into thin circles. Arrange the orange and onion slices, overlapping, on the platter and spoon over the vinaigrette dressing.

Eggplant Boston – eggplant slices, onion and ham are layered with béchamel sauce before browning

VEGETABLE ENTREES

Vegetables should not always play second fiddle to meat; not only are vegetables a great source of unusual appetizers like stuffed zucchini or cauliflower au gratin, but many economical entrées can be made from them too. Try eggplant galette, layered with yogurt and tomato sauce, or cabbage leaves stuffed with rice, mushrooms and hard-cooked eggs for a tempting lunch or supper suggestion.

Serve globe artichoke with melted butter, vinaigrette dressing or mayonnaise

Globe Artichokes

To boil: cut the stalk of the artichoke level with the base and trim the leaves and top with scissors to remove the spines. Wash thoroughly, then cook the prepared artichokes in boiling salted water for 25—45 minutes, depending on size. When one of the leaves can be pulled away easily, the artichoke is ready. Drain thoroughly and serve hot with melted butter, flavored with tarragon if you like, or serve cold with vinaigrette dressing or mayonnaise.

To eat globe artichokes: pull off the leaves, one by one, and dip the fleshy ends into melted butter, vinaigrette dressing or mayonnaise; discard the leaf after eating the tip. Pull off all the leaves until the 'choke' appears. Gently scrape away these hairy fronds from the bottom and discard. Pour a little melted butter or dressing on the bottom, season and eat this part with a knife and fork.

If a leaf pulls away easily, the artichoke is cooked

Italian Stuffed Artichokes

4 large globe artichokes
1 cup white wine
1 cup beef stock

For filling
1 onion, chopped
2 tablespoons olive oil
4 anchovy fillets, soaked in 2 tablespoons milk
½ cup fresh white breadcrumbs
2 cloves of garlic, crushed
¼ cup green olives, pitted and chopped
1 teaspoon oregano
1 tablespoon chopped parsley
juice of ½ lemon
black pepper, freshly ground

Method
Prepare the artichokes as directed, left, and cook in boiling salted water for 35–40 minutes. Drain, discard some of the inner leaves and scoop out the hairy center 'choke' with a teaspoon.

To make the filling: fry the onion in oil until soft. Drain the anchovy fillets and chop them. Combine onion and anchovy with the remaining ingredients and season well with pepper.

Fill the artichoke cavities with stuffing and tie a string around the leaves to prevent them from falling open. Set the artichokes in a deep casserole, pour over the wine and stock and bake in a moderate oven (350°F) for 35–45 minutes or until the artichokes are very tender, basting occasionally.

Serve the artichokes hot or cold in bowls with the cooking liquid spooned over them.

Eggplant Soufflé

2 medium eggplants
¼ cup oil
1 cup white sauce, made with 3 tablespoons butter, 3 tablespoons flour, 1 cup milk, salt, pepper and nutmeg
5 egg yolks
¼ cup grated Parmesan cheese
8 egg whites
2 tablespoons grated Parmesan cheese, 2–3 tablespoons browned breadcrumbs (for sprinkling)

Soufflé dish (1½ quart capacity)

Method
Wrap a strip of foil or silicone paper around the dish so it comes 1½ inches above the top of the dish; tie with string to make a collar. Thickly butter inside the dish and collar, and sprinkle with browned breadcrumbs, discarding the excess. Set oven at hot (425°F).

Wipe the eggplants, trim the stems and cut them in half, lengthwise. Run the point of a knife around the inside of the skin and score the flesh. Sprinkle with salt and leave 30 minutes to draw out the bitter juices (dégorger). Rinse with cold water to remove the salt and dry on paper towels.

In a skillet or flameproof casserole, heat the oil and fry the eggplants, cut side down, until brown. Transfer to a moderately hot oven (375°F) and bake 10–15 minutes or until tender. Scoop out the flesh and purée it in a blender or work through a sieve.

Make the white sauce, take from heat and stir in the eggplant purée. Add yolks one at a time and stir over low heat until the mixture thickens. Take from heat, stir in the

¼ cup cheese and adjust seasoning.

Whip the egg whites until they hold a stiff peak and, using a metal spoon, fold one-quarter into the eggplant mixture to lighten it. Add remaining egg whites and fold together as lightly as possible. Transfer the mixture to the soufflé dish, sprinkle with cheese and breadcrumbs and bake at once in heated oven for 15–20 minutes or until puffed and brown. Remove collar and serve at once.

To prepare a soufflé dish: rub inside with butter, and sprinkle with browned crumbs for a savory soufflé. Wrap around a band of paper with 2 inch fold at the base and 3 inch overlap at top. Tie securely with string to hold the collar in place

Dégorger means to remove impurities and strong flavors before cooking. Either soak the food, e.g. uncooked ham, in cold water for specified length of time, or sprinkle sliced vegetables, e.g. cucumber, eggplant etc., with salt, cover with a heavy plate and leave for 1 hour. Wash away salt.

Eggplant Boston

2 medium eggplants, sliced
6 tablespoons olive oil
1 medium onion, chopped
2 tablespoons butter
salt and pepper
1 cup (½ lb) cooked ham, cut in strips
1½ cups béchamel sauce (see page 43)
1 tablespoon cream (optional)
¼ cup grated Gruyère or Cheddar cheese

Method
Sprinkle the eggplant slices with salt and leave 30 minutes to draw out the bitter juices (dégorger). Rinse with cold water to remove the salt and dry on paper towels.

Place the eggplant slices on an oiled baking sheet, brush with oil and bake in a moderate oven (350°F) for 15 minutes or until beginning to brown. Turn over, brush again with oil and cook 10 minutes longer or until brown also.

Cook the onion in the butter until soft and mix with the ham.

In a casserole or baking dish, arrange the eggplant slices overlapping in layers with the onion and ham and coat each layer with béchamel sauce, ending with a layer of sauce. Sprinkle with grated cheese and bake in a hot oven (400°F) for 15–20 minutes or until the top is golden brown.

After cooling, turn out the cooked eggplant galette

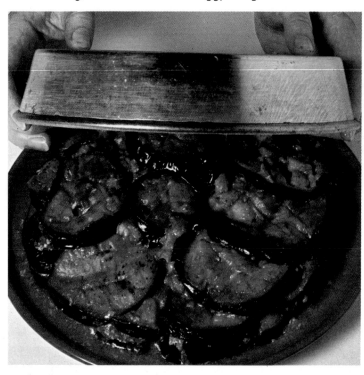

Eggplant Galette

3–4 small eggplants
½ cup olive oil
1 clove of garlic, crushed
1 medium onion, finely
   chopped
3 tomatoes, peeled, seeded and
   chopped, or 2 cups (1 lb)
   canned Italian-type plum
   tomatoes
1 tablespoon tomato paste
salt and pepper
1 cup plain yogurt
¼ cup stock

*8 inch moule à manqué, or
   springform pan (2–2½ quart
   capacity)*

Method
Wipe the eggplants, trim the stems and cut in diagonal slices. Sprinkle with salt and leave 30 minutes to draw out the juices (dégorger). Rinse with cold water and dry on paper towels.

In a saucepan heat 2 table-spoons of the oil, add garlic and onion and fry slowly until the onion is golden. Add tomatoes and tomato paste, season and cook 10–15 minutes or until the mixture is thick and pulpy.

Heat the remaining oil and brown the eggplant slices on both sides. Arrange a layer of eggplant slices in the pan, spread with a little tomato mixture and yogurt and continue in layers until all the eggplant is used, ending with a layer of eggplant. Reserve about one-third of the tomato mixture and stir in stock to make a sauce.

Cover the eggplant with foil, press down lightly and bake in a moderate oven (350°F) for 40–45 minutes or until the eggplant is very tender. Cool a few minutes, then turn out. Heat the tomato sauce, spoon over the galette and serve.

Stuffed Zucchini 1

6–8 medium zucchini
2 tablespoons butter
1 onion, chopped
1 clove of garlic, crushed
1 cup (¼ lb) chopped
   mushrooms
1 cup (½ lb) ground cooked
   beef, or any cooked meat
pinch of allspice
1 egg, beaten to mix
salt and pepper
1 cup grated Parmesan or
   Cheddar cheese

This recipe can also be made with scallop or straightneck yellow squash.

Method
Wash the zucchini, trim the stems and blanch in boiling water for 5 minutes. Drain, refresh with cold water, drain again and cut in half lengthwise. Scoop out the pulp from the center and reserve.

In a skillet melt butter and fry the onion until golden. Add the garlic and mushrooms and cook over medium heat until the moisture has evaporated. Take from heat and stir in the ground beef or other cooked meat. Add zucchini pulp, all-spice and egg and season well.

Pile the mixture into the zucchini shells and sprinkle with cheese. Bake in a moderately hot oven (375°F) for 30 minutes or until the zucchini are tender and brown. Serve plain or with tomato sauce (see page 41).

Stuffed Zucchini 2

6–8 medium zucchini
2 tablespoons butter
1 onion, chopped
1 clove of garlic, crushed
3 tomatoes, peeled, seeded and
   chopped
8–10 anchovy fillets, soaked in
   ¼ cup milk to remove excess
   salt, drained and chopped
1 teaspoon basil
1 tablespoon chopped parsley
salt and pepper

Method
Prepare zucchini as for stuffed zucchini 1.

In a skillet heat butter, fry onion until soft, add remaining ingredients with zucchini pulp and salt and pepper to taste. Fill and bake zucchini as previous recipe.

Stuffed Tomatoes

4 large tomatoes, halved
   crosswise
2 tablespoons butter
1 onion, chopped
1 clove of garlic, crushed
¼ cup fresh white breadcrumbs
1 tablespoon chopped parsley
salt and pepper

Serve as a garnish with stuffed zucchini.

Method
In a skillet heat the butter and fry the onion until soft. Stir in garlic, breadcrumbs, parsley and salt and pepper.

Squeeze the tomatoes gently to remove most of the seeds and fill them with the onion mixture. Bake them in a moderately hot oven (375°F) with stuffed zucchini for 10–15 minutes or until tender and browned.

Stuffed onions, with tomato sauce spooned around, are garnished with sprigs of fresh rosemary

Stuffed Onions

6–8 mild or Bermuda onions
1½ cups tomato sauce (see
    page 41)
2 teaspoons fresh rosemary
    or 1 teaspoon dried rosemary
sprigs of fresh rosemary
    (for garnish) – optional

For stuffing
1 lb ground beef
½ cup fresh white breadcrumbs
grated rind of ½ lemon
1 clove of garlic, crushed
salt and pepper
1 egg, beaten to mix
1–2 tablespoons milk

Method
Cook the onions, without peeling them, in boiling salted water for 15–20 minutes or until almost tender. Drain them, peel and trim the root. Scoop out the centers with a teaspoon, leaving enough of the root to form a base, and finely chop the flesh from the center.

To make the stuffing: mix the ground beef, breadcrumbs, lemon rind, garlic and chopped onion and season well. Stir in the beaten egg and enough milk to bind the mixture and season.

Put enough of the stuffing into the onions to fill them, doming the tops. Stir the remaining stuffing into the tomato sauce with the chopped rosemary.

Spread the tomato mixture in a shallow baking dish and set the onions in it. Bake them in a moderately hot oven (375°F) for 15–20 minutes or until lightly browned. Garnish each onion with a sprig of fresh rosemary, if you like.

Spinach Mold

1½ lb fresh spinach or 2
    packages frozen spinach
3 tablespoons butter
½ cup fresh white breadcrumbs
½ cup hot milk
1 egg
1 egg yolk
salt and pepper
3 tablespoons browned bread-
    crumbs (for sprinkling)
1–2 cups (¼–½ lb) mushrooms,
    sautéed in butter
8–12 slices of crisply fried
    bacon (for garnish)
2 cups mornay sauce

Plain mold (3–4 cup capacity)

Method
Wash the fresh spinach well, remove the tough stems and cook in plenty of boiling salted water for 5 minutes or until tender; or cook frozen spinach according to package directions. Drain spinach thoroughly and press to remove the water. Work through a food mill or purée in a blender.

Melt the butter in a pan, add the spinach and cook 3–4 minutes, stirring, until the moisture has evaporated and the purée is firm. Cool.

Soak the fresh breadcrumbs in the hot milk and add to the spinach with the egg and egg yolk, beaten to mix, and seasoning.

Butter the mold, sprinkle with the browned breadcrumbs and put in the spinach mixture. Cover with buttered foil, stand in a water bath and bake in a moderate oven (350°F) for 45–55 minutes or until the mold is firm to the touch. Remove from water bath and leave 2–3 minutes; turn out onto a platter.

Surround spinach mold with sautéed mushrooms and crisp bacon and serve the mornay sauce separately.

Mornay Sauce

For 2 cups: melt 3 tablespoons butter in a pan and stir in 3 tablespoons flour off the heat. Pour in 2 cups milk and bring to a boil, stirring. Simmer 2 minutes, season and cool a little before beating in ¼ cup grated Gruyère or Cheddar cheese. Stir in ½ teaspoon Dijon-style or prepared mustard and seasonings to taste.

Watchpoint: when using Dijon-style mustard, be careful not to boil the sauce after adding the mustard as this spoils the taste.

Brazilian Corn Casserole

2 cups corn kernels, cooked
    and drained
1 tablespoon butter
1 tablespoon flour
1 cup milk
3 eggs, separated
½ teaspoon sugar
salt and pepper
¼ cup chopped cooked ham
¼ cup seedless raisins

Soufflé dish (1½ quart capacity),
or 8 individual molds

Method
Generously butter the dish or molds; set the oven at moderately hot (375°F).

In a pan melt the butter, stir in the flour off the heat and pour in the milk. Bring to a boil, stirring, and simmer 2 minutes. Take from the heat, stir in the corn kernels with the egg yolks, sugar and seasoning to taste. For a smooth-textured casserole, purée the mixture in a blender. Stir in the ham and raisins.

Whip the egg whites until they hold a stiff peak, carefully fold into the corn mixture with a metal spoon.

Transfer the mixture to the soufflé dish or molds and cover with buttered foil. Bake the small molds in heated oven for 20 minutes and the soufflé dish for 30–40 minutes or until a knife inserted in center comes out clean. Turn out individual molds onto a platter before serving, but serve the large mold in the soufflé dish.

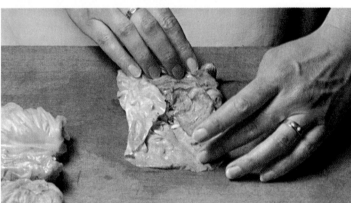

Left: for stuffed cabbage leaves, place a spoonful of filling on each cooked leaf

Center: fold the leaf edges into the center and roll up like a small package

Below left: roll each cabbage package very lightly in flour before packing into the pot

Stuffed Cabbage Leaves

1 head of green cabbage
2 teaspoons flour

For filling
6 tablespoons rice
1 medium onion, finely chopped
2 tablespoons butter
1 cup ($\frac{1}{4}$ lb) finely chopped mushrooms
2 hard-cooked eggs, finely chopped
salt and pepper

For sauce
1$\frac{1}{2}$ cups vegetable stock
2 teaspoons tomato paste
kneaded butter, made with 2 tablespoons butter and 1 tablespoon flour
2 tomatoes, peeled, seeded and cut in strips

Method

Cook rice in plenty of boiling salted water for 10–12 minutes or until tender. Drain, rinse in hot water and drain again.

Wash the cabbage, trim the stalk and put cabbage in a large kettle of boiling salted water. Simmer, uncovered, for 3–4 minutes. Lift out and peel off the outer leaves. When the leaves become difficult to detach, put the cabbage back into boiling water until all are separated. Discard the core and trim the stalks level with the bases of leaves.

To make the filling: cook the onion in the butter until soft. In a bowl mix the onion, mushrooms, rice and eggs and season well.

Place a spoonful of filling on each leaf and roll up like a package. Roll each one lightly in the flour and pack into a deep flameproof casserole or pan.

Watchpoint: arrange the packages at an angle so they do not squash each other.

Pour over enough stock to cover, bring to a boil, cover with the lid or a piece of buttered foil and simmer on top of the stove or in a moderately low oven (325°F) for about 45 minutes. Pour off the stock into a pan, stir tomato paste into it and thicken by bringing to a boil and stirring in the kneaded butter a little at a time. Simmer 2 minutes, add tomato strips and heat for 1 minute. Arrange packages in a serving dish or leave in the casserole, spoon over the sauce and serve.

Lemon Stuffed Cabbage

1 head of green cabbage

For lemon stuffing
grated rind of $\frac{1}{2}$ lemon
$\frac{1}{4}$ cup butter
1 onion, finely chopped
$\frac{1}{2}$ cup fresh white breadcrumbs
1 tablespoon chopped parsley
2 eggs, beaten to mix
salt and pepper

For garnish
1$\frac{1}{2}$ cups tomato sauce
2 tablespoons fresh white
  breadcrumbs
1 tablespoon butter

Medium heatproof bowl

Lemon stuffed cabbage can also be cooked as individual leaves. For detaching and stuffing the leaves, follow the instructions for stuffed cabbage leaves and make the lemon stuffing as below. Pack the leaves into a deep pan, cover them with boiling salted water, add the lid and simmer 30–35 minutes or until the packages are firm. Drain them and serve as in the following recipe.

Method

Wash the cabbage well and trim the stem. Cook in a large pan of boiling salted water for 3–4 minutes and drain.

Remove 6 outside leaves. Line the bowl with damp cheesecloth and arrange the cabbage leaves in it, stalks upright.

To make the stuffing: shred or finely chop the remaining cabbage, discarding any hard stalks. Melt the butter in a shallow pan, add the onion and chopped or shredded cabbage, cover and cook over very low heat for 10 minutes or until the cabbage is tender, stirring occasionally. In a bowl, combine the cabbage mixture with $\frac{1}{2}$ cup breadcrumbs, parsley, beaten eggs and lemon rind and season well.
Watchpoint: be sure the mixture is not too wet; if the eggs are large, add only enough to moisten the mixture.

Spoon the mixture into the bowl lined with cabbage leaves. Bring the edges of the cheesecloth together and tie up firmly in a ball. Immerse the ball in a large pan of boiling salted water and simmer 45–60 minutes or until the mixture is firm.

Meanwhile make the tomato sauce; fry the breadcrumbs in the butter until golden brown.

To serve, lift the cabbage ball carefully from the pan, drain and untie the cheesecloth. Set the ball, stalk side down, on a hot serving dish and spoon tomato sauce around or serve separately, if you like. Sprinkle breadcrumbs on top. Cut in wedges for serving.

Tomato Sauce

Melt 2 tablespoons butter in a pan, stir in 1$\frac{1}{2}$ tablespoons flour and blend in 1$\frac{1}{2}$ cups stock or water, off the heat. Bring to a boil, stirring.

Cut 2 cups tomatoes (1 lb can or 4 fresh tomatoes) in half and squeeze to remove seeds. (Peel fresh tomatoes only if you will be puréeing in a blender.) Strain the seeds to remove the juice. Add tomatoes and juice to the sauce with bouquet garni. Season, add a pinch of sugar and 1 teaspoon tomato paste to strengthen the flavor, if you like. Cover the pan and simmer gently for 30 minutes or until tomatoes are pulpy. Remove bouquet garni. Work the sauce through a strainer or purée in a blender. Return to the rinsed pan and adjust seasoning; simmer 5 minutes or until it is the right consistency.
Note: a tomato sauce should be of flowing, rather than coating consistency. For a good gloss, stir in 1 tablespoon butter before serving.

Cauliflower with Mushrooms

1 large cauliflower
1 bay leaf
1 tablespoon browned
  breadcrumbs
1 tablespoon melted butter

For mushroom mixture
2 cups ($\frac{1}{2}$ lb) mushrooms
2 cups milk, or 1 cup milk and
  1 cup water mixed
3 tablespoons butter
2 tablespoons flour
salt and pepper

Method

Remove the mushroom stalks, chop them and simmer in the milk or milk and water in a covered pan for 30 minutes. Strain and reserve the liquid.

Wash the cauliflower thoroughly in salted water. Trim the stalk, leaving a few of the small green leaves, and cook with the bay leaf in boiling salted water, head down, for 8–10 minutes or until the flower part is tender. Drain carefully and cut out the thick part of the stalk. Set the cauliflower upright in a baking dish.

To prepare the sauce: slice or quarter the mushroom caps and cook them in 1 tablespoon butter until tender. Lift out, melt the remaining butter in the pan, stir in the flour off the heat and pour on the mushroom-flavored milk or milk and water. Bring to a boil, stirring, season and simmer 2 minutes.

Cut a few flowerets from the center of the cauliflower and fill the center with mushrooms. Replace the flowerets and spoon the sauce over and around the cauliflower. Sprinkle breadcrumbs on top, then the melted butter and bake in a hot oven (400°F) for 10 minutes or until browned.

Lemon stuffed cabbage may be served as individual stuffed leaves with tomato sauce served separately, if you like (recipe is on page 41)

Vegetables in Béchamel Sauce

For this attractive dish, choose at least 3–4 vegetables of contrasting colors and textures. Cook them as directed below, arrange in an ovenproof dish and cover with buttered foil to keep hot, or to reheat before serving.

Use either recipe for béchamel sauce; the long method is particularly suitable when the vegetables are to be served alone as an entrée because the flavor of the sauce is very delicate. Just before serving, spoon over the sauce — it should be very creamy and just thin enough for the shape and color of the vegetables to show through.

Cauliflower: break it into flowerets and cook, uncovered, in boiling salted water for 8–10 minutes or until just tender. Drain, refresh with cold water, drain again and stir gently for 1–2 minutes over low heat with a little melted butter.

When boiling cauliflower add a bay leaf; this lessens the strong smell and gives a delicate flavor to the vegetable.

Brussels sprouts: trim these neatly and cook as for cauliflower for 10–12 minutes.

Carrots: trim, peel and keep them whole if young, otherwise quarter them lengthwise. For about 1 lb carrots, add $\frac{1}{2}$ teaspoon salt, $\frac{1}{2}$ teaspoon sugar and 1 tablespoon butter and barely cover with cold water. Cook the carrots in a covered pan until tender, remove the lid, boil until the water has completely evaporated, leaving a sticky glaze. Sprinkle with a little finely chopped mint or parsley.

Small onions: for about 10–15 onions ($\frac{1}{2}$ lb), peel, blanch for 2 minutes, drain and cook slowly, covered, with 1 tablespoon butter and 1 teaspoon sugar for 8–10 minutes or until onions are brown, sticky and tender. Shake pan occasionally.

Mushrooms: trim the stems level with the caps and keep them whole if small or quarter them if large. Sauté mushrooms quickly in butter with a squeeze of lemon juice, then drain on paper towels.

Whole cherry tomatoes: first scald and peel, then cook, covered, over low heat in a little butter for 3 minutes or until just cooked but still firm. Shake pan often so that they are evenly coated with butter.

Celery: wash stalks, cut into 3 inch lengths, tie in bundles and cook in boiling salted water for 15–18 minutes or until tender. Drain well, remove the strings and pour over a little melted butter.

Béchamel Sauce

Louis de Béchamel (the Marquis de Nointel) was Lord Steward to the Royal household of Louis XIV. Béchamel sauce is said to have been named after him rather than created by him. It is an important sauce because, like ordinary white sauce, it forms the base for many others (see Volume 2). To make it, the milk is infused with seasonings and flavorings to give a delicate taste. Recipes vary slightly according to what the sauce is used for — here are the two basic methods, one short and a longer one with a more subtle flavor.

Long Method

$2\frac{1}{2}$ cups milk
bouquet garni
salt and pepper
pinch of ground nutmeg
1 tablespoon light cream (optional)

For mirepoix
2 tablespoons butter
1 small onion, diced
1 small carrot, diced
$\frac{1}{2}$ stalk of celery, diced

For roux
2 tablespoons butter
2 tablespoons flour

Makes 2 cups.

Method
Melt the butter for the mirepoix in a large heavy pan, add the diced vegetables and press a piece of buttered foil on top. Cover and sweat 8–10 minutes, i.e. cook the vegetables gently without letting them brown. Turn the mirepoix out onto a plate.

To make the roux: in the same pan melt the butter, stir in the flour off the heat and pour in one-third of the milk. Scald remaining milk and add to the sauce, whisking well. Add bouquet garni, seasoning and nutmeg and bring to a boil, whisking constantly. Add mirepoix, half cover the pan and simmer over low heat, stirring occasionally, for 40 minutes.

Strain the sauce into a clean pan, pressing the vegetables lightly to remove the juice. Reheat and add the cream, if you like.

Short Method

2 cups milk
slice of onion
6 peppercorns
1 blade of mace
1 bay leaf
salt and pepper
1 tablespoon light cream (optional)

For roux
2 tablespoons butter
2 tablespoons flour

Makes 2 cups.

Method
Infuse the milk with the onion and seasonings in a covered pan by scalding and keeping over very low heat for 5–7 minutes — do not boil. Strain the milk.

To make the roux: melt the butter, remove the pan from the heat and stir in the flour. Strain in at least one-third of the milk and blend with a whisk or wooden spoon. Strain in the remaining milk, season lightly, return to the heat and bring to a boil, stirring constantly. Simmer 2 minutes, then taste for seasoning. If you like, add 1 tablespoon cream.

Your cocktail parties will be transformed when you try this galaxy of canapés varying from stuffed grapes, roulades of smoked salmon, dried beef rolls, to stuffed olive canapés and lobster boats. Fill tiny cream puffs with clam dip or chicken and mushrooms; roll miniature pancakes around bacon rolls or stuff them with cream cheese and red caviar. Top cheese pastry canapés with stuffed olives and chutney. Make tartlets niçoise with delicious cheese pastry, or shrimps in cheese sauce.

These are just some of the hot and cold canapés and dips you will find on the next few pages. Choose a selection from them to make a good contrast in color, flavor and texture, and then go on to deal with cocktail drinks like a professional and follow the expert's advice in a bartender's guide (see page 56).

GIVING A COCKTAIL PARTY

Selection of Canapés

Stuffed Grapes
Roulades of Smoked Salmon
Stuffed Cherry Tomatoes
Stacked Sandwiches
Dried Beef Rolls   Asparagus Tartlets
Stuffed Olive Canapés
Roulades   Lobster Boats
Smoked Cod's Roe with Salted Almonds
Tartlets Niçoise
Cream Cheese & Tart Jelly Rounds
Cream Cheese & Smoked Salmon Rounds
Chive Pastries   Savory Choux
Clam Dip   Shrimps Mariette
Savory Pancakes
Mushroom Beignets
with Devil Sauce Dip
Cheese Straws

❧

Cocktails (see page 56)

Cocktail Hors d'Oeuvre

Eye appeal is essential when serving hors d'œuvre. To present the food effectively, make one large table with a centerpiece as the focal point and then arrange an attractive selection of canapés and dips around it. For instance, choose the most handsome pineapple you can find and set it in the middle of a large platter. Attach as many cooked, peeled shrimps on toothpicks as the pineapple will comfortably hold and surround it with crackers, potato chips and bowls of dips for the shrimps.

Arrange canapés in rows or circles on large trays to make a lavish spread and decorate platters with plenty of watercress and colorful vegetables like tomatoes.

Since it is quicker and easier to make a large quantity of one item rather than small quantities of several different kinds, choose just a few from the wide variety of basic pastries and fillings given here. Be sure the canapés are fresh and lightly seasoned to balance the piquancy of cocktails.

For most cocktail parties, caterers allow four canapés per person, plus salted nuts, potato chips, crackers and one or two dips.

For convenient-sized **cocktail canapés** use 2 inch long boat molds and tartlet tins measuring $1\frac{1}{4}$—$1\frac{3}{4}$ inches in diameter. Quantities are for these sizes.

How to make a Paper Decorating Cone for Piping

1 Fold a 10 inch square of wax or silicone paper; cut into 2 triangles. Hold 1 triangle with center point up, fold 1 point over to meet center point.

2 Fold the other point around the back to form a cone.

3 Fold over the flap formed where all points meet the top of the cone; crease

firmly with a fingernail to prevent it from unfolding. Snip a little piece from the point and use plain, or drop in a decorating tube before adding the mixture to be piped.

COLD HORS D'OEUVRES

Stuffed Grapes

1 lb large black grapes
1 small package (3 oz) cream cheese
salt and black pepper
2 tablespoons finely chopped salted browned almonds

Paper decorating cone and a small star tube

Makes about 30 according to size of grapes.

Method
Rinse the grapes, pat dry with paper towels and carefully remove from stems. Make shallow splits in the stem ends of the grapes and lift out seeds with a pointed knife or rounded end of a sterilized bobby pin.

Work the cream cheese with salt and pepper to taste and put in paper decorating cone fitted with a small star tube. Fill the grapes generously with seasoned cheese. Dip the tops into the chopped almonds to cover them lightly on top. If you like, spear each grape with a toothpick.

Roulades of Smoked Salmon

1 small unsliced loaf of wholewheat bread
$\frac{1}{2}$ cup butter, softened
$\frac{1}{2}$ lb smoked salmon, very thinly sliced
juice of $\frac{1}{2}$ lemon
black pepper, freshly ground

Method
Cut the crust lengthwise from the top of the loaf. Spread the surface of the bread with butter and cut a thin slice the length of the loaf. Continue buttering and slicing until the bottom crust is reached. Cover each slice with a layer of smoked salmon and season with lemon juice and freshly ground pepper. Trim off the crusts and roll each slice

the length of the loaf (like a jelly roll). Cut each roll into thin slices.

Watchpoint: if the bread is crumbly after the slice is rolled with the seasoned salmon, wrap the rolls in wax paper and chill them in the refrigerator. Cut in neat thin slices.

Dried Beef Rolls

$\frac{1}{2}$ lb dried beef, thinly sliced
2 packages (3 oz each) cream cheese, softened
1 tablespoon prepared horseradish (or to taste)

Method
Separate the slices of dried beef carefully. Spread each slice with cream cheese mixed with the horseradish. Roll up the beef like a jelly roll and cut into pieces about $1\frac{1}{2}$–2 inches in length. Fasten each little beef roll with a toothpick.

Stuffed Cherry Tomatoes 1

1 box (1 pint) cherry tomatoes

For caviar filling
small jar of black caviar
juice of $\frac{1}{2}$ lemon
finely chopped hard-cooked egg white (optional)

Method
Wash the cherry tomatoes and pat dry with paper towels. With a sharp, pointed knife cut a slice from the stem end. Use a demitasse spoon to hollow out a little of the tomato flesh.

Spoon a little caviar into each cavity, add a squeeze of lemon juice and, if you like, sprinkle with egg white.

From left to right: asparagus tartlets, stuffed grapes and smoked salmon roulades

Stuffed Cherry Tomatoes 2

Soften a 3 oz package of cream cheese and beat in enough milk or cream to make a smooth soft mixture. Season well and spoon into a pastry bag or paper decorating cone and small plain tube. Hollow out cherry tomatoes as before, fill with cream cheese mixture and dip the tops in finely chopped chives.

Cheese Straws

$\frac{1}{2}$ cup grated Parmesan or dry Cheddar cheese
6 tablespoons butter
1 cup flour
1 egg yolk
1–2 teaspoons water

Makes 35–40 straws.

Method
Set oven at moderately hot (375°F).

Cut the butter into the flour, then rub with the fingertips until the mixture resembles crumbs. Add the cheese and egg yolk, lightly beaten with the water, and continue working to form as smooth a dough as possible. Chill at least 1 hour before rolling out to about $\frac{1}{4}$ inch thickness. Cut into even strips $\frac{1}{4}$ inch wide and 4 inches long. Shape 6 strips into rings and leave the remainder flat. Lay on a baking sheet and bake in heated oven for 12–15 minutes or until golden.

When cold, lift the straws from the baking sheet and slip 4–5 into each ring. Arrange them carefully on a platter because they are very fragile and break easily.

Stacked sandwiches can be made with a variety of fillings; secure them with toothpicks

Stacked Sandwiches

Make sandwiches using thinly sliced bread. With a cookie cutter, cut 3–4 small round sandwiches from each large one. Sandwich 2 small sandwiches with any chosen ingredient (see below), also cut in a circle if necessary, and finish with a circle of bread. Secure the stacked sandwiches with toothpicks and garnish with sprigs of parsley, if you like.

California: sandwich white bread with sliced tongue or ham, sliced tomato and a mixture of equal quantities of chopped ripe olives, chopped walnuts and pecans with enough mayonnaise to bind.

Egg and cheese: sandwich pumpernickel bread with layers of thinly sliced Gruyère cheese and hard-cooked egg, chopped and mixed with mayonnaise to bind and chopped dill pickles to flavor.

Ham and pâté: sandwich wholewheat bread with layers of liver pâté and ham.

Ham and salami: sandwich white bread with layers of ham, salami, sliced tomato.

Neuchâtel: sandwich rye bread with sliced Gruyère cheese and finely chopped cooked ham or tongue, bound with mayonnaise and well seasoned with Dijon-style mustard.

Smoked salmon: sandwich wholewheat bread with layers of smoked salmon, cream cheese softened with a little milk and flavored with finely chopped onion or fresh chives, and red or black caviar, mixed with sour cream to bind.

Savory Cheese Pastry

1 cup flour
salt and pepper
large pinch of cayenne
$\frac{1}{4}$ cup shortening
2 tablespoons grated Parmesan cheese
1 egg yolk, mixed with $\frac{1}{2}$–1 tablespoon water

Use this pastry for canapés and small boat and tartlet molds. This quantity makes about 24–30 canapé rounds ($1\frac{1}{4}$ inch diameter), or 12–15 boat or tartlet molds. The pastry recipe can be doubled satisfactorily.

Method
Set oven at moderately hot (375°F).

Sift the flour into a bowl with the salt, pepper and cayenne. Rub in the shortening with the fingertips until the mixture resembles crumbs. Stir in the cheese and gradually add the egg yolk mixture. Work lightly to make a dough and chill at least 30 minutes.

On a lightly floured board, roll out the dough until about $\frac{1}{4}$ inch thick and cut into rounds $1\frac{1}{4}$ inches in diameter. Or line the pastry into the boat or tartlet molds (see page 50). Place on a baking sheet lined with foil or silicone paper and bake in heated oven for 7–8 minutes or until lightly browned.

Watchpoint: do not put this kind of cheese pastry directly on the baking sheet. Such small canapés can easily become too brown in a very short time – in the time it takes to lift the first half-dozen from the baking sheet, the remaining pastries can scorch. By lifting the foil or silicone paper straight from the hot baking sheet to a cooling rack you can remove all the pastries at once.

Stuffed Olive Canapés

1 cup quantity of savory cheese pastry, cut into 24 rounds and baked
24 large green olives
24 anchovy fillets

For savory butter
$\frac{1}{4}$ cup unsalted butter
2 teaspoons chutney, finely chopped
2 hard-cooked eggs
salt and pepper

To decorate
$\frac{1}{4}$ cup unsalted butter
1 teaspoon anchovy paste (or to taste)
few drops of red food coloring (optional)

2 paper decorating cones and a small star tube

Method
To make the savory butter: cream the butter and beat in the chutney and egg yolks to make a smooth paste. Season well with salt and pepper.

To pit olives: make a small cut across the top of the olive (not all the way through). Keeping the blade of the knife against the pit, cut in a spiral pattern removing flesh as you cut. Remove flesh from the bottom of the pit and the pitted olive will retain its shape.

Spread a little savory butter on each canapé; put remaining butter in a small paper decorating cone and snip off the tip. Pipe savory butter into each olive. Place a stuffed olive in the center of each canapé and shape an anchovy fillet around it.

For decoration: mix the butter together with anchovy paste to taste and tint with a little red food coloring, if you like. Put into the second paper decorating cone fitted with the star tube, and pipe a tiny rosette on the top of each olive.

Note: the egg white can be chopped and sprinkled on top of the olive, or it can be reserved for decorating other canapés.

Roulades

2 cup quantity of savory cheese pastry
1 tablespoon Dijon-style mustard
1 tablespoon paprika
1 tablespoon anchovy paste
1–2 tablespoons grated Parmesan cheese

Makes about 75 roulades.

Method
Roll out the cheese pastry to about one-eighth inch thickness; spread with a thin layer of mustard; sprinkle with paprika, spread with anchovy paste and sprinkle with cheese.

Roll the pastry as for a jelly roll, wrap it in wax paper and chill for at least 30 minutes. Slice the roll into $\frac{1}{4}$ inch slices, thinner if possible, and lay them on a baking sheet lined with foil or silicone paper. Bake roulades in a moderately hot oven (375°F) for about 8 minutes or until lightly browned. Remove roulades all at once (on the paper) from the baking sheet.

Quantity Terms
Terms like 1 cup quantity of pastry (or 2 cup quantity) refer to the amount obtained by using 1 cup (or 2 cups) flour NOT 1 cup prepared dough.

Smoked Cod's Roe with Salted Almonds

1 cup quantity of savory cheese
   pastry (see page 49), cut
   into 24 rounds and baked
¾ cup (7½ oz jar) smoked cod's
   roe, or tarama (smoked
   fish roe)
2 tablespoons butter
¼ cup heavy cream
24 browned whole salted
   almonds (for garnish)

*Pastry bag and a small plain
tube*

Tarama or smoked fish roe is
available in Danish and Middle
Eastern specialty stores.
Makes about 24 canapés.

Method
Cream the butter and beat in
the roe or pound the mixture
in a mortar and pestle. Work
it through a sieve. Beat in the
heavy cream and work until
the mixture is smooth. If you
like, purée it in a blender.

Using a pastry bag fitted
with the plain tube, pipe the
mixture onto the top of each
cooked pastry round. Add a
salted almond for decoration.

Lobster Boats

2 cup quantity of savory cheese
   pastry (see page 49)
1 cup (½ lb) cooked lobster
   meat, fresh or canned
¼ cup vinaigrette dressing
½ cup finely chopped celery
1 tablespoon chopped parsley
3–4 tablespoons mayonnaise
¼ cup chopped watercress

Makes 24–30 boats.

Method
Cut the lobster meat into small
pieces and let marinate in the
vinaigrette dressing while
baking boat molds of cheese
pastry.

Drain the lobster and mix it
well with the celery and
parsley. Stir in just enough
mayonnaise to bind the mixture together and spoon it
into the boat molds. Sprinkle
the tops with the chopped
watercress.

Asparagus Tartlets

2 cup quantity of savory cheese
   pastry (see page 49)

For filling
1 bunch of fresh asparagus
   (about 24 spears), or
   2 packages frozen asparagus,
   cooked
3–4 tablespoons vinaigrette
   dressing

2 teaspoons chopped mixed
   herbs (chives, parsley,
   tarragon)
2 small packages (3 oz each)
   cream cheese
salt and pepper

24–30 small boat molds

Method
Roll out the savory cheese
pastry dough and line the boat
molds (see below). Bake them
blind and cool pastry boats

How to make Pastry Boats and Tartlet Shells

Houseware sections of large department stores or kitchen specialty shops
often carry interesting tiny boat and
tartlet molds made of tin. The most
practical size boat mold is 2 inches long,
and the best tartlet tins are 1¼–1¾ inches
in diameter. These small shapes make a
canapé that is one mouthful.

To line the molds with dough, arrange
the molds close together near the pastry
board. Roll out the dough on the board
until just under ¼ inch thick. Lift onto
the rolling pin and lay gently on top of the
molds. Take a small piece of dough and
dip it in flour. Use this to work the dough
down into each boat or tartlet mold.

Take the rolling pin and roll it over the
tops of the little molds. This neatly cuts
the pastry off the top of each one. Lift up
each tin mold and pat the pastry down
with your thumb dipped in flour.

Put a small piece of wax paper or foil,
crumpled, and a few grains of rice into
each mold. Paper and rice hold the
pastry in position while it bakes. Bake
blind in a moderately hot oven (375°F)
for about 8 minutes or until the pastry
is lightly browned. Remove the paper and
rice and leave the pastry shells until
nearly cold before removing them from
the molds.

before removing from molds.

Drain the cooked asparagus on paper towels. Trim each spear to the size of a pastry boat. Spoon vinaigrette dressing and the mixed herbs over the asparagus and let stand to absorb the flavors.

Soften the cream cheese and beat in salt and pepper to taste. Spoon it into the pastry boats, leveling the cheese with a small spatula. Arrange a spear of asparagus,

drained of dressing, on top of the cheese in the pastry boat.

Quantity Terms
Terms like 1 cup quantity of pastry (or 2 cup quantity) refer to the amount obtained by using 1 cup (or 2 cups) flour NOT 1 cup prepared dough.

Shown in the selection of canapés are, from left to right in vertical rows: (first row, front to back) stuffed cherry tomatoes, tartlets niçoise (fillings 1 and 2) and stuffed grapes; (second row) lobster boat, savory pancakes stuffed with cream cheese and caviar; (third row) tartlets niçoise (filling 2) with roulades between; (fourth row) tartlet niçoise (filling 3) and savory pancakes stuffed with cream cheese and caviar; and finally, stuffed grapes, tartlet niçoise (filling 1) and stuffed cherry tomatoes

Tartlets Niçoise

2 cup quantity of savory cheese pastry makes 24–30 tartlets; bake in appropriate molds or tins. Various fillings are suitable for these tartlets; here are three alternatives. Filling 1 is for round tartlets and fillings 2 and 3 are for pastry boat molds; each is enough for 24–30 tartlets.

Filling 1

1 can sardines in oil
2 tablespoons vinaigrette
   dressing
1 tablespoon capers, chopped

For garnish
12–15 cherry tomatoes, peeled
   and halved

Method
Drain sardines thoroughly, discarding any skin and bone, if you like. Mash sardines and stir in vinaigrette dressing and capers. Fill baked pastry tartlets with the mixture, leveling the tops. Cover each tartlet with a halved tomato.

Filling 2

½ cup creamed cottage cheese
2 tablespoons butter
salt and pepper
8 ripe olives, pitted and finely
   chopped

For garnish
2 hard-cooked eggs

Method
Work the cottage cheese with the butter until well mixed. Stir in the chopped olives and season to taste. Fill baked pastry boats with the mixture, piling it high; shape into an inverted 'V' with the blade of a knife. Arrange sieved

egg yolk down one side and finely chopped egg white down the other.

Filling 3

1 clove of garlic, cut in half
¾ cup unsalted butter
¼ cup tomato paste
salt and pepper (to taste)
sugar (to taste)
squeeze of lemon juice

For garnish
2 tablespoons finely chopped
   parsley
2 tablespoons finely chopped
   browned almonds

Method
Rub a small bowl with the garlic, add the butter and work until creamy. Stir in tomato paste, seasoning, sugar and lemon juice.

Fill the baked pastry boats with the mixture. Pile it high, then shape it into an inverted 'V' with the blade of a knife. Place the chopped parsley along one side of 'V' and the almonds along the other.

Cream Cheese and Tart Jelly Rounds

1 cup quantity of savory almond
   pastry
2 packages (3 oz each) cream
   cheese
¼ cup butter, softened
2 tablespoons hot milk
salt
4–6 tablespoons tart jelly (red
   currant, guava or quince)

*Pastry bag and a small star
   tube*

Makes about 24–30 canapés.

Method
Bake the pastry in 1¼ inch rounds.

Beat the cheese and butter together, adding the hot milk gradually to make the mixture the right consistency for piping. Season to taste with salt.

Put the cheese mixture into the pastry bag fitted with the

Use savory cheese pastry to make tempting lobster boats and tartlets niçoise

star tube and pipe it around the edges of the pastry rounds. Spoon the jelly into the center of the round.

Watchpoint: to prevent the jelly from softening too much, scoop it from the jar with a small salt spoon or tip of a teaspoon. Place the scoops in the center of each canapé.

Cream Cheese and Smoked Salmon Rounds

1 cup quantity of savory
   almond pastry
2 packages (3 oz each) cream
   cheese
¼ lb smoked salmon, sliced and
   chopped
salt and pepper
black pepper, freshly ground
1–2 tablespoons hot milk
juice of ½ lemon

*Pastry bag and a small star
   tube*

Makes about 18 canapés.

Method
Set oven at moderately hot (375°F).

Roll out the almond pastry dough to ¼ inch thickness on a lightly floured board and cut it into 2 X 1 inch rectangles. Bake in heated oven for 5–6 minutes; cool.

Work the cream cheese with the salt and black pepper and enough hot milk to make the mixture the right consistency for piping. Fill into the pastry bag fitted with the star tube.

Season the chopped salmon with black pepper and a

little lemon juice. Pipe the cream cheese mixture on the top of each cooked pastry rectangle and sprinkle with chopped salmon.

Savory Almond Pastry

1 cup flour
salt and pepper
pinch of cayenne
$\frac{1}{4}$ cup shortening
2 tablespoons whole blanched almonds, ground
1 egg yolk, mixed with $\frac{1}{2}$–1 tablespoon water

This quantity makes about 24–30 canapé rounds $1\frac{1}{4}$ inches in diameter, or 12–15 boat or tartlet molds. The pastry recipe can be doubled satisfactorily.

Method
Set oven at moderately hot (375°F).

Sift the flour into a bowl with the salt, pepper and cayenne. Rub in the shortening until the mixture resembles crumbs. Stir in the ground almonds and gradually add the egg yolk mixture. Work the mixture lightly to make a dough and chill at least 30 minutes before using. Shape and bake as for savory cheese pastry (see page 49).

pastry (see page 49).

Quantity Terms
Terms like 1 cup quantity of pastry (or 2 cup quantity) refer to the amount obtained by using 1 cup (or 2 cups) flour NOT 1 cup prepared dough.

HOT HORS D'OEUVRES

Chive Pastries

2 cups flour
salt and pepper
pinch of cayenne
$\frac{1}{4}$ cup butter
$1\frac{1}{2}$ tablespoons chopped chives
1 egg, beaten to mix
$\frac{1}{2}$ cup milk
little milk or beaten egg (for brushing)

$1\frac{1}{2}$ inch cookie cutter

These small savory pastries are good served hot to accompany a savory dip. Makes about 50 pastries.

Method
Set oven at hot (400°F).

Sift the flour with the salt, pepper and cayenne, rub in the butter with the fingertips until the mixture resembles crumbs and mix in the chopped chives. Stir the egg into the flour mixture and gradually add enough milk to make a soft dough. Put the dough on a lightly floured board and knead lightly to make a smooth ball. Roll out to a little less than $\frac{1}{2}$ inch thickness and cut into rounds with the cookie cutter.

Place the rounds on an ungreased baking sheet, brush the tops with milk or beaten egg and bake in heated oven for 10–12 minutes.

Clam Dip

$1\frac{1}{2}$ tablespoons chopped shallots or scallions
$\frac{1}{4}$ cup butter
1 cup chopped fresh or canned clams, drained
$\frac{1}{3}$ cup dry white wine
salt and pepper
1 teaspoon tarragon
2 tablespoons flour
1 cup milk or 1 cup milk and clam juice (mixed)
1 egg yolk
$\frac{1}{4}$ cup heavy cream
$\frac{1}{4}$ cup grated Gruyère cheese

Method
Cook shallots or scallions in half the butter over low heat for 1 minute or until soft. Stir in the clams and cook slowly for about 2 minutes. Pour in the wine and cook over a high heat until almost all the liquid has evaporated. Season to taste and stir in the tarragon.

In a separate saucepan heat the remaining butter and stir in the flour until smooth; cook for about 1 minute. Take pan from heat and stir in the milk or milk and clam juice. Season with salt and pepper to taste and cook stirring, until the sauce thickens. Simmer 2 minutes and take from heat.

In a bowl beat the egg yolk and cream. Beat a little of the sauce into the yolk mixture, then pour this into the rest of the sauce. Return to the saucepan and heat until the sauce thickens slightly but do not boil. Add the onion and clam mixture and grated cheese and taste for seasoning.

Serve hot or cold with chive pastries or spooned into savory choux (see page 55).

Mushroom Beignets with Devil Sauce Dip

4 cups (1 lb) small firm mushrooms
fritter batter (made with $\frac{1}{4}$ cup flour, pinch of salt, 2 egg yolks, 1 tablespoon melted butter or oil, $\frac{1}{2}$ cup milk, 1 egg white)
deep fat (for frying)
fried parsley (for garnish)

For devil sauce dip
1 cup mayonnaise
1 tablespoon finely chopped sweet pickles
1 tablespoon finely chopped parsley
1 clove of garlic, crushed
1 teaspoon grated onion
1 tablespoon chopped capers
1 tablespoon chopped olives
salt and pepper

Method
Trim the mushroom stems level with the caps and wipe mushrooms with a damp cloth.

Prepare the fritter batter (see Volume 3), cover with plastic wrap and let stand for 30 minutes.

Combine all ingredients for the devil sauce dip and season well.

Dip each mushroom into the batter and fry in hot deep fat (350°F on fat thermometer). Do not crowd the pan. When the batter coating is crisp and golden brown, remove the mushrooms with a slotted spoon and drain on paper towels. Garnish with fried parsley and serve hot, speared on toothpicks. Serve the devil sauce dip in a separate bowl.

Shrimps Mariette are a delicious hot hors d'oeuvre

Shrimps Mariette

½ lb canned or frozen baby
   shrimps, cooked, drained
   and peeled
20–24 rounds of white bread,
   1–1½ inches in diameter
½ cup butter
salt
pinch of pepper, cayenne or
   few drops of Tabasco

For thick mornay sauce
2 tablespoons butter
2 tablespoons flour
1 cup milk
¾ cup grated dry Cheddar or
   Gruyère cheese
dry mustard (to taste)

Method

Heat half the butter in a skillet and fry the rounds of bread, a few at a time, on both sides until they are golden brown. Drain and keep warm. Add more butter as necessary.

In a saucepan combine the shrimps with the seasonings and remaining butter and cook, shaking the pan frequently, until the shrimps are heated through. Place shrimps on top of the fried bread rounds, set them in an ovenproof dish and keep warm.

To make the thick mornay sauce: melt the butter in a small saucepan, remove from heat and stir in the flour until smooth. Add the milk and cook over a low heat, stirring constantly, until the sauce thickens. Simmer 3 minutes, take from heat, and gradually stir in the grated cheese. Season lightly and add dry mustard to taste.

Spoon a little mornay sauce over the prepared shrimps and put under the broiler until well browned. Serve very hot.

Savory Pancakes

1 cup flour
salt and pepper
pinch of cayenne
1 teaspoon sugar
2 tablespoons grated Parmesan
   cheese
1 egg
2 tablespoons melted butter
¾ cup milk

These quick pancakes are at their best when filled at the last moment. This amount of batter makes about 24 pancakes. Some suggested fillings follow; each is enough for about 24 pancakes.

54

Method

Heat a griddle or heavy skillet over moderate heat while mixing the batter.

To make the batter: sift the flour, seasonings and sugar into a bowl. Thoroughly mix in the Parmesan cheese. Make a well in the center, drop in the egg and the melted butter, and stir in the milk gradually, beating well with a wooden spoon or whisk to form a smooth batter.

Lightly grease the griddle or skillet and pour the batter from the point of a spoon to make a small round pancake. As soon as they are puffy, full of bubbles and golden brown underneath, turn them with a small spatula and brown the other side.

Serve the pancakes immediately, or place between the folds of a clean warm dish towel until serving. Do not reheat the pancakes because they will become tough.

Filling 1

1 package (3 oz) cream cheese, softened
salt and pepper
1 small jar red caviar
squeeze of lemon juice

Method

Season the cream cheese with salt and pepper to taste and spread it on the hot pancakes.

Sprinkle the caviar generously with lemon juice and put about $\frac{1}{2}$ teaspoon caviar in the center of each pancake. Fold over and fasten with a toothpick.

Filling 2

Cut 12 slices of bacon in half, roll them up and spear them on a skewer. Bake bacon rolls in a moderate oven (350°F) or broil until brown and crisp. Remove from the skewer and, while both the bacon and the pancake are still hot, curve the pancake around the bacon roll and fasten with a toothpick.

Filling 3

For a really elegant cocktail hors d'œuvre put 1 teaspoon pâté de foie gras on each warm pancake and fold it over; fasten with a toothpick.

A less expensive but good alternative is to use liver pâté: lightly season it with a little Dijon-style mustard and add a few drops of brandy.

Savory Choux
(Miniature Cream Puffs)

$\frac{1}{2}$ cup water
$\frac{1}{4}$ cup butter
$\frac{1}{2}$ cup flour
salt and pepper
pinch of cayenne
2 large eggs
little beaten egg
1–2 tablespoons grated Parmesan cheese

Pastry bag and a $\frac{1}{4}$ inch plain tube

These cream puffs should be filled and reheated at the last minute. This quantity of pastry makes about 30 little puffs.

Method

Set oven at hot (400°F).

To make choux pastry dough: put the water and butter into a saucepan. Sift the flour and seasonings onto a piece of wax paper. Bring the water and butter mixture to a boil. When bubbling, draw the pan from heat and immediately stir in the flour all at once. Stir vigorously until the mixture is smooth.

Cool the mixture for about 5 minutes, then beat in the eggs, one at a time, beating hard after each addition; then beat for about 3 minutes until the dough looks glossy.

Put the dough into the pastry bag fitted with the plain tube and pipe little mounds about 1 inch in diameter and $\frac{1}{2}$ inch high on a dampened baking sheet. Space the mounds 2 inches apart. Brush the top of each mound with a little beaten egg and sprinkle with Parmesan cheese.

Bake in heated oven for about 15 minutes or until the puffs are brown and very crisp to the touch. Remove from the oven and while still hot make a small slit in the side of each puff with a sharp knife to release the steam. Let them cool completely.

Fill the puffs, using the pastry bag fitted with the $\frac{1}{4}$ inch plain tube if the filling is smooth. Otherwise split the puffs and fill with a teaspoon. Two suggested fillings are given right or use the clam dip (see page 53).

Filling 1

$\frac{3}{4}$ cup finely chopped cooked chicken
1 cup ($\frac{1}{4}$ lb) very finely chopped mushrooms
3 tablespoons butter
2 tablespoons flour
1 cup milk
$\frac{1}{2}$ teaspoon tarragon
salt and pepper

Method

In a saucepan melt the butter and add the mushrooms. Cook for about 2 minutes or until all moisture has evaporated. Stir in the flour off the heat. Add the milk, cook over moderate heat, stirring constantly, until the sauce thickens. Simmer 2 minutes and take from the heat.

Add the cooked chicken, tarragon and seasoning, and fill the puffs with the chicken and mushroom mixture. Place the puffs in a baking dish and heat in a moderately low oven (325°F) for 8–10 minutes.

Filling 2

$\frac{1}{2}$ cup very finely chopped ham
$\frac{1}{4}$ cup grated Parmesan cheese
3 tablespoons butter
2 tablespoons flour
1 cup milk
salt and pepper

Method

In a saucepan melt the butter and stir in the flour off the heat. Add the milk and cook over moderate heat, stirring constantly, until the sauce thickens. Simmer 2 minutes and take from the heat.

Stir in the ham and cheese and season with salt and pepper to taste. Fill the puffs with the ham and cheese mixture. Place the puffs in a baking dish and heat in a moderately low oven (325°F) for 8–10 minutes.

A BARTENDER'S GUIDE

One reason for the continuing popularity of the cocktail party is that it is easy to give. Far less demanding than a dinner, the hosts have only two things to prepare for their guests — good drinks and some interesting edibles to go with them. But even a cocktail party needs careful preparation. The following list may help.

1 Glasses. For whatever drinks you intend to serve ensure that you have the appropriate glassware, spotlessly clean and in greater number than your guests (somebody is sure to 'lose', break or simply want a fresh glass as the party progresses). Normally, a set of Old Fashioned and Highball glasses, plus some sort of stemware for the Martinis and Manhattans will suffice.

2 Hardware. The host should be prepared with the requisite tools for opening bottles and mixing drinks. At a minimum, these include a corkscrew, a cap remover, a jigger for measuring, a long handled bar-spoon and stirrer and a good sharp knife for cutting, bottle seals, slicing lemons, spearing olives, etc. Ice picks and tongs, strainers, fruit squeezers and muddlers are in the 'nice to have' category.

3 Ice. It is difficult to have too much ice. We like our drinks *cold* and in recent years the preference for having nearly every drink 'on the rocks' has grown enormously. In summer, of course, the demand for ice is particularly high as tastes turn to those taller drinks involving tonic, Collins mix, bitter lemon, etc. To be sure you have enough ice, compute the quantity needed for the number of drinks you expect to serve — and double it.

4 Mixers. The most important companion for alcohol is water. Sad to say, the chlorine and other chemicals added to city water supplies and the high iron content of water in some rural areas can make water from the tap a poor mixer. If this is the case where you live, bottled spring water is something to consider. The carbonated mixers you may want will depend largely upon the season, but club soda is in demand all year.

5 'Garbage'. This indelicate, but widely accepted, term for the fruits and vegetables with which drinks are garnished is well deserved, since few are actually consumed and they usually end up in the trash. Nevertheless, they do have an important role to play in the appearance of a drink and sometimes contribute significantly to its flavor. Freshness is a must and the bartender will find his task easier if these items are prepared beforehand — the lemons sliced, the olives extracted from their bottles — and all arranged in small, readily accessible bowls; this also saves time.

6 Quantities. You know your friends and how much liquor they are likely to consume. As a general rule, however, 3 drinks per person over a 2 hour cocktail party should be more than ample.

Quick
Cocktail Guide

Each cocktail serves 1 person.

Bullshot: 2 oz vodka, 1 oz lemon juice, 4 oz beef consommé. Shake with cracked ice, strain into an 8 oz chilled glass; add ice cubes.

Champagne Cocktail: in chilled 6 oz Champagne glass, put strip of lemon rind, cube of sugar and 1 oz brandy. Fill with chilled Champagne.

Daiquiri: 2 oz light rum, 1 oz lime juice, 1 teaspoon superfine (bar) sugar. Shake well with cracked ice; strain into a 4 oz chilled glass.

Gin Fizz: 2 oz gin, 1 oz lemon juice, 1 teaspoon superfine (bar) sugar. Shake with cracked ice and strain into a 6 oz chilled glass. Fill with club soda and stir.

Manhattan: 2 oz blended whiskey, 1 oz sweet vermouth, dash of bitters. Stir well with cracked ice and strain into a 4 oz chilled glass. Serve with a Maraschino cherry.

Martini: 2 oz gin, $\frac{1}{2}$ oz dry vermouth. Pour gin over cracked ice, stir in vermouth (add more or less as you like) and strain into a chilled 3 oz glass. Add an olive or a twist of lemon rind.

Mint Julep: crush several sprigs of fresh mint in the bottom of an 8 oz glass with 1 teaspoon superfine (bar) sugar and a dash of cold water. When mint is well bruised and sugar is dissolved, pack glass with shaved ice and add 3 oz bourbon. Stir well, repack with shaved ice and decorate with a sprig of mint.

Old Fashioned: in a 4 oz chilled glass, dissolve 1 teaspoon superfine (bar) sugar in 2 dashes of bitters and 1 tablespoon water. Stir, add ice cubes and 2 oz blended bourbon, or Scotch. Stir well and add a slice of orange, twist of lemon and a cherry.

Tom Collins: 2 oz gin, 1 oz lemon juice, 1 teaspoon superfine (bar) sugar. Shake well with cracked ice, strain into a 12 oz chilled glass, add ice cubes, fill with club soda and stir. Add a slice of orange, twist of lemon and a cherry.

Whiskey Sour: 2 oz bourbon or blended whiskey, 1 oz lemon juice, $\frac{1}{2}$ teaspoon superfine (bar) sugar. Shake with cracked ice, strain into a 4 oz glass and add a slice of lemon and a cherry.

Recipes for Bloody Mary and Screwdriver were in Volume 3.

A selection of homemade breads: light rolls, wholewheat and fine wholewheat loaves (left) and cottage loaves (right)

HOW TO MAKE BREAD

Few foods give more pleasure than the taste and smell of freshly baked bread, and it is easy to make once you understand the use of its ingredients. Yeast, the most important ingredient, is a living plant and must be treated carefully, but otherwise bread is not tricky. Making bread has the reputation of being tedious, but the actual time needed for working and shaping the dough is quite short, with more time occupied by rising and baking.

Homemade bread does not keep as well as commercial kinds that contain preservatives, but fresh bread freezes well and unbaked dough can be shaped, then frozen for 2–3 weeks before baking.

Points to remember

1 Kneading the dough helps make the bread light; this is an important stage of bread-making because the kneading distributes the yeast evenly. To knead by hand, place the dough on a floured board, take the edge of dough and pull into the center with the fingers. Push out again with the heel of the hand so that the dough rolls on the board; use both hands in a rhythmical movement.

2 At the beginning, the dough will take up flour, so keep the board well coated to prevent the dough from sticking. After 3–5 minutes, the dough will start peeling from the board in one piece and, after kneading a few minutes longer, it will have reached the correct smooth, elastic texture. Most bread-makers find kneading the most satisfying part of bread-making, but if you want to save work, some electric mixers have a dough hook that can be set at low speed to knead the dough for you.

3 Crust finishes. For a crisp crust on regular breads, leave the loaves as they are. The water in the recipe helps to make a crisp crust. For a soft crust, rub with butter after baking while the loaves are still hot, then cover with a cloth and leave 5–10 minutes.

Richer doughs, such as those for coffeecakes and rolls, contain fat and eggs; they have a naturally soft crust and the inside has a spongy texture.

For a crisper crust on these breads, brush the tops before baking with a little milk or with 1 egg beaten with 1 tablespoon milk.

Ingredients for Bread

Yeast is a living plant that needs warmth and moisture to grow. It is affected by extremes of temperature — excess cold will retard or check (but not kill) the growth; strong heat will kill it completely. Because of this, bread dough can be mixed and stored before the second rising, either in the refrigerator for a short period or in the freezer for a longer time.

After the long and slow rising process, when the dough is risen and light, bread is baked in a hot oven to kill the yeast as fast as possible.

Yeast is sold dry in packages or compressed in cakes and is date-stamped to show its life-span. Instructions for using yeast are given on the package — normally **dry yeast** is sprinkled over a few tablespoons of warm liquid and left to dissolve.

Compressed yeast can be dissolved in warm liquid or it can be softened with sugar.

Both kinds of yeast should be kept in the refrigerator; for long periods of time store compressed yeast in the freezer.

The proportion of yeast to flour affects the rising time.

The smaller the quantity of yeast, the longer the rising will take — the greater the quantity of yeast, the shorter the rising time. Proportions of yeast to flour also vary with the type of bread.

Regular breads: 1 package active dry (or 1 cake compressed) yeast to 6 cups flour.

Light or milk breads: 1 package (or 1 cake) yeast to 4–5 cups flour.

Rolls: 1 package (or 1 cake) yeast to 3 cups flour.

Sugar helps yeast to grow and when they are creamed together they quickly become liquid. However, take care not to overmix them as this retards the action of the yeast.

Salt retards growth if mixed with yeast, so salt is usually sifted with the flour or dissolved in part of the liquid.

Flour: all-purpose flour is used for most breads and wholewheat or graham flour can be added to make darker, heavier breads. As its name implies, wholewheat flour is milled from the whole grain wheat. It is neither refined nor bleached. It can also be

used in close-textured quick breads and muffins. Some small mills produce stone-ground flour which is ideal for bread-making; it can be found in health food stores and in some supermarkets. Special bread flour with a high gluten content produces bread that is particularly moist and spongy. Bread flour is sold in a few specialty stores. Flours made from other grains, such as rye, are also often used in breads.

Note: detailed information on types of flour was given in Volume 1.

Stages in Bread-making

There are four distinct stages when making bread.

1 Sponging. This helps to speed up the general rising of the dough and produces a fine grain in the finished bread. It is only used for some breads.

Sift the flour into a warm bowl with the salt, make a well in the center and add all the liquid in which the yeast has been dissolved.

Draw in enough flour from

Kissing crust is the name sometimes incorrectly given to the pale soft crust formed where one loaf has touched another in baking.

Traditionally, it refers to the soft cracks that appear on the surface of the loaves when they are left to cool.

BAKING TEMPERATURES

Type	Oven Temperature
Regular breads	400°F–425°F
Rolls	425°F
Coffeecakes	400°F–425°F
Brioche, savarin, rich coffeecakes	400°F

the sides of the well to make a thick batter. Generously sprinkle the top of the batter with flour taken from the sides, cover with a damp cloth and set in a warm, draft-free place to rise — near a radiator, over the stove's pilot light or anywhere with a temperature around 75°F–80°F.

Leave the dough for 15–20 minutes or until bubbles start to break through the surface, showing the batter has started to rise. The batter or sponge, as it has now become, is ready for the next stage. (In many breads, such as whole-wheat bread, this sponging step is eliminated and the dough rises for the first time as in Stage 2).

2 Rising. Draw the rest of the flour into the dough and knead it well on a board or work surface, adding enough flour to make a dough that is soft but not sticky. In any bread recipe, flour quantities are approximate: because liquid in the recipe is absorbed more readily by some flours than by others, do not follow quantities blindly.

Transfer the dough to a warm lightly greased bowl, turning it over so the top surface is lightly coated with grease (this prevents a skin from forming). Cover the bowl with a damp cloth, set it in a warm, draft-free place and leave 1 hour or more or until doubled in bulk.

When fully risen, the dough will not spring back if a finger is inserted in it. A steamy atmosphere (between 70°F–80°F) helps the rising. The dough is then ready for shaping.

3 Second Rising. This stage is a short period of rising that comes after the dough is shaped and placed in loaf pans or on a baking sheet. Put

For sponging, work all the yeast liquid into flour that has been sifted into a warm bowl

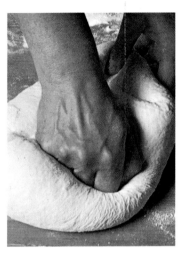
After the batter starts to rise, work in the remaining flour, and knead the dough well

After kneading until dough is soft but not sticky, put it into a lightly greased bowl to rise

When the dough is doubled in size, turn it out of the bowl and onto a floured board

Knead the dough lightly again, then shape and put it into the greased loaf pans

Leave pans in a warm place to let dough rise again until almost doubled in size

the dough in a slightly warmer place than for the first rising — the temperature should be about 80°F–85°F; leave 10–15 minutes or until the dough swells to almost double its bulk. A few breads, such as cracked wheat bread and Sally Lunn, rise only once and at this third stage.

4 Baking. As soon as the dough has risen well, put it into the heated oven. As a general rule, all yeast mixtures are baked in a hot oven; for specific temperatures, see chart, left.

When done, yeast breads sound hollow when tapped.

White Bread

6 cups all-purpose or bread
    flour
2 cups water
2 teaspoons salt
1 package dry or 1 cake
    compressed yeast
$\frac{1}{2}$ teaspoon sugar

*2 large loaf pans (9 X 5 X 3
inches)*

Method
Warm the water to lukewarm
(90°F–100°F).

Sift the flour with the salt
into a warm mixing bowl.
Stir the compressed yeast
gently with sugar until creamy
or dissolve the dry yeast in
a few tablespoons of the lukewarm water. Add remaining
water to the yeast with the
sugar if not already added.

Make a well in the center of
the flour and pour in the yeast
mixture. Draw in enough flour
to make a thick batter and
sprinkle the top generously
with flour from the sides.
Cover the bowl with a damp
cloth and leave to rise in a
warm place for 15–20
minutes.

When bubbles have started
to break through the floured
surface, work the mixture to a
dough with your hand. Turn it
onto a floured board and
knead 7–10 minutes or until
the dough is smooth and
elastic, sprinkling the board
with flour when necessary to
prevent it from sticking.

Put the dough back into a
clean and lightly greased
warm bowl, turn the dough
over and make a shallow
crosscut on the top. Cover
with the cloth and leave to
rise for 1–1$\frac{1}{2}$ hours or until
doubled in bulk.

Grease the loaf pans and
set oven at hot (425°F).

Turn the dough out onto the
floured board and knead
lightly for a few seconds. Then
cut in half, shape by folding
under the edges of the dough
so the top is very smooth and
put into the pans, smooth side
up.

Stand the pans on a baking
sheet, cover with a cloth and
leave 15–20 minutes in a
warm place until almost
doubled in bulk. Bake in
heated oven for 20–25
minutes, lower the temperature to 400°F and bake 15–20
minutes longer.

When the bread is well
browned and shrinks slightly
from the sides of the pan, tap
the loaves — if they sound
hollow, the bread is done.
Cool on a wire rack.

Cottage Loaf

Make as for white bread, but
when shaping the dough
before the second rising,
divide it into 2 pieces, one
twice the size of the other.
Knead each piece lightly into
a ball. Set the large piece on a
greased baking sheet, put the
smaller one on top and push a
finger through the center,
straight down almost to
baking sheet. Let rise and
bake as for white bread.

Simple
Coffeecake

You can make a simple coffeecake from white bread dough
by working in dried fruit,
butter, sugar and eggs before
the final rising.

When making white bread,
reserve half the dough and
work in $\frac{1}{4}$ cup creamed butter,
1–2 eggs, $\frac{1}{2}$ cup dried fruit
and $\frac{1}{4}$ cup sugar or to taste.

Shape the dough into a
ball, folding it to the center,
then turning it upside down
so it is plump and high. Cover,
let rise and bake as for white
bread.

To finish: brush the bread
with 1–2 tablespoons melted
apricot jam glaze and sprinkle
with 2 tablespoons finely
chopped candied fruits and
raisins, mixed, and 6 cubes of
sugar, crushed. To crush the
sugar, tie it in a double piece
of cheesecloth or the corner of
a dish towel and pound it with
a hammer or rolling pin.

Rich Coffeecake

5 cups flour
$\frac{1}{2}$ teaspoon salt
pinch each of ground cinnamon,
    allspice, nutmeg and cloves
6 tablespoons butter
1$\frac{1}{2}$ cups milk
1$\frac{1}{2}$ packages dry or 1$\frac{1}{2}$ cakes
    compressed yeast
2 teaspoons sugar
3 eggs
$\frac{1}{2}$ cup currants
$\frac{1}{2}$ cup golden raisins
3 tablespoons finely chopped
    mixed candied peel
6 tablespoons sugar
grated rind of $\frac{1}{2}$ lemon
1 tablespoon sugar, dissolved
    in 1 tablespoon milk (for
    glaze)

*2 large loaf pans (9 X 5 X 3
inches)*

Method
Grease the loaf pans.

Sift the flour, salt and
spices together into a warm
bowl. Heat the butter and
milk together until the butter
melts and let cool to lukewarm. Cream the compressed
yeast with the 2 teaspoons
sugar or dissolve the dry
yeast in a little of the lukewarm milk and butter. Beat in
the eggs and add the mixture
to the remaining milk with the
2 teaspoons sugar, if not
already added.

Make a well in the flour,
pour in the yeast, egg and
milk mixture and mix to a soft
dough. Knead on a generously
floured board until smooth.
Put in a greased bowl, cover
with a damp cloth and let rise
in a warm place for 45 minutes
or until doubled in bulk.

Set oven at hot (400°F).

Mix the dried and candied
fruits into the dough with the
6 tablespoons sugar and
lemon rind. When well mixed,
shape and put into the greased
pans. Cover with a damp
cloth and let rise again in a
warm place for 15–20 min-
utes or until almost doubled
in bulk.

Bake in heated oven for
35–40 minutes or until the
coffeecake is brown and
sounds hollow when tapped.
Brush with sweetened milk
and return to oven for 1–2
minutes to dry the glaze. Cool
on a wire rack.

Simple coffeecake, made with white bread dough, is finished with candied fruits, raisins and crushed sugar

English Muffins

4 cups flour
1 teaspoon salt
1 package dry or 1 cake
  compressed yeast
½ cup lukewarm milk
2 teaspoons sugar
1 cup warm water
¼ cup butter, softened

4–5 inch cookie cutter

Makes 16–18 muffins.

Method
Sift the flour with the salt. In a large bowl, sprinkle the yeast over the milk and leave 5 minutes or until dissolved. Add the sugar and water and gradually beat in 2 cups flour. Cover the bowl and let stand in a warm place for 1½ hours or until the mixture rises and then collapses back into the bowl. Beat in the softened butter and add most of the remaining flour.

Turn the dough out onto a floured board and knead in the remaining flour until the dough is smooth and elastic. Put it in a greased bowl, cover with a damp cloth and let rise again in a warm place until doubled in bulk.

On a lightly floured board, pat or roll out the dough to ½ inch thickness; cut into 4–5 inch rounds with the cutter. Let stand in a warm place for 20 minutes or until doubled in bulk.

Cook the muffins on a lightly oiled griddle or skillet over moderate heat for 5–7 minutes on each side or until brown. Cool on a wire rack.

Before serving, halve the muffins with a fork, not a knife, as an uneven surface toasts better. Toast, and spread with butter for serving.

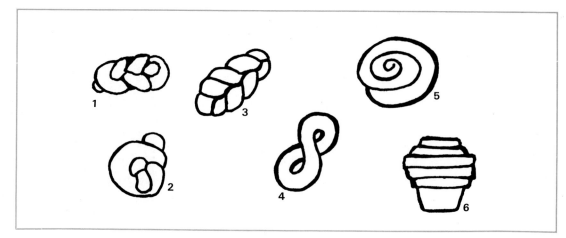

Shaping Rolls
1 Baker's knot: roll each piece into a 10 inch rope. Make a figure eight, tuck in each end. 2 Bow knot: roll each piece of dough into a rope 9–10 inches long. Make a very loose knot. 3 Braid: make as for large light bread loaf on page 67. 4 Figure eight: roll each piece into a rope about 10 inches long. Pinch the ends together; twist to form a figure eight. 5 Snail: roll each piece into a rope 10 inches long. Start winding the strip around and tuck the end firmly underneath. 6 Fan slices: roll dough ¼ inch thick and cut into 6 strips. Lay one on top of the other, cut in squares and set horizontally in a muffin tin

To Bake Rolls

Set oven at hot (425°F). Shape the rolls and brush, if you like, with a little milk for a crisp crust, or 1 egg yolk, beaten with 1 tablespoon water, for a glaze. Bake the rolls in heated oven for 15–20 minutes or until they are brown and sound hollow when tapped. Cool on a wire rack.

Martha's Coffeecake

4½ cups flour
1 teaspoon salt
2 cups milk
½ cup butter
1½ packages dry or 1½
  cakes compressed yeast
¼ cup sugar
2 eggs, beaten to mix
¾ cup raisins
¾ cup golden raisins
¾ cup coarsely chopped
  dates
¾ cup candied cherries

For icing
½ cup confectioners' sugar
1½ teaspoons water

*2 medium loaf pans
(8½ X 4½ X 2½ inches)*

This coffeecake keeps well for several weeks in an airtight container.

Method
Add 2 tablespoons of the flour to the fruit and mix well – this prevents the fruit from sinking to the bottom of the cake. Grease the pans.

Sift the remaining flour with the salt into a mixing bowl. Heat the milk and butter until lukewarm, sprinkle or crumble over the yeast and let stand 5 minutes or until dissolved. Stir in the sugar and beaten eggs.

Make a well in the center of the flour and pour in the yeast mixture. Mix to a smooth batter with the hand and beat for 5 minutes or until the dough is shiny and elastic. Cover with a damp cloth and let rise in a warm place for 1½ hours or until doubled in bulk.

Set oven at hot (400°F).

Knead the dough lightly to knock out air and work in the raisins, dates and candied cherries. Transfer the dough to the prepared pans. Let rise again in a warm place for 30 minutes or until almost doubled in bulk.

Bake in heated oven for 40–45 minutes or until the bread sounds hollow when tapped; cool on a wire rack.

To make the icing: mix the confectioners' sugar with enough water to make a pourable mixture and brush it over the bread while still warm.

Martha's coffeecake, made with raisins, dates and candied cherries, is finished with a little icing

Light Bread

5 cups flour
1½ teaspoons salt
1½ cups milk
¼ cup butter
1 package dry or 1 cake
   compressed yeast
1½ teaspoons sugar
1 large egg, beaten to mix

To finish
1 egg, beaten with ½ teaspoon
   salt (for glaze)
1 tablespoon poppy seeds
   (optional)

*1 large loaf pan (9 X 5 X 3
inches) or 2 medium pans
(8½ X 4½ X 2½ inches)*

Method

Sift the flour and salt into a warm bowl. Warm the milk slightly, add the butter and stir until melted. Cream the compressed yeast gently with sugar or dissolve the dry yeast in a little of the warm milk. Add the remaining milk to the yeast with the egg and sugar, if not already added.

Make a well in the center of the flour, pour in the yeast, egg and milk mixture and mix with your hand to a soft dough. Turn out onto a floured board and knead well until smooth and elastic. Put in a greased bowl, turn the dough over and cover with a damp cloth. Leave in a warm place to rise for 1 hour or until doubled in bulk.

Set oven at hot (400°F) for loaves and braids.

Turn the dough onto a floured board and knead lightly. For loaves, shape into 1 large or 2 medium balls and set in greased loaf pans. If making 1 loaf, use remaining dough for rolls.

For a braid, shape the dough to a cylinder, and leaving one end joined, cut it in three lengthwise, braid it and turn

under the loose ends.

Let dough rise again in a warm place until almost doubled in bulk, then brush with egg glaze. Sprinkle with poppy seeds before baking, if you like. Bake the loaves or braids in heated oven for 40–45 minutes or until they are brown and hollow-sounding when tapped. Cool the bread on a wire rack.

Wholewheat Bread

5–6 cups wholewheat flour,
   preferably stone-ground
2½ cups mixed milk and water
1 tablespoon salt
1½ teaspoons dark brown sugar
1 package dry or 1 cake
   compressed yeast

*Two 8 inch round cake pans
(optional)*

Method

Warm the milk and water mixture to lukewarm.

Sift the flour thoroughly with the salt into a warm mixing bowl and make a well in the center. Gently stir the sugar into the compressed yeast until creamy or dissolve the dry yeast in a little of the warm milk and water. Add the remaining milk and water to the yeast with the sugar, if not already added, and stir well.

Pour the yeast mixture into the well and mix the flour into the liquid with your hand, gradually drawing it from around the sides of the bowl. The dough should be softer than for white bread; work only until well mixed, not until it is elastic. Cover the bowl with a thick damp cloth and let rise in a warm place for 1–1½ hours or until doubled in bulk.

Set oven at hot (400°F) and grease the pans, if using.

Turn the dough onto a floured board and knead until it comes away cleanly from the board and your hands. Divide dough in two, knead each piece until there is no trace of stickiness.

Shape each piece into a round loaf and put on a floured baking sheet or into the pans, but do not let the sides of the loaves touch the pan sides. Let rise again in a warm place for about 30 minutes or until the dough has almost doubled in bulk. Bake in heated oven for 1 hour or until the bread sounds hollow when tapped. Cool on a wire rack.

Fine Wholewheat Bread

5 cups wholewheat flour
1½ cups all-purpose flour
2 teaspoons salt
2 tablespoons butter or
   shortening
1 package dry or 1 cake
   compressed yeast
1 teaspoon sugar
2–2¼ cups warm water

*2 large loaf pans (9 X 5 X 3
inches) or two 9 inch cake
pans*

Method

Sift the flours and salt together into a warm bowl and rub in the butter or shortening. Continue and finish as for wholewheat bread, using floured baking sheets, or loaf or cake pans.

For a **peaked finish** on bread, after brushing with glaze, snip the surface diagonally with a large pair of scissors and lift the cut edges into peaks.

Stuffed white bread, filled with a mixture of almond paste and candied cherries, is a good breakfast coffeecake

Stuffed White Bread

A good breakfast coffeecake can be made by rolling regular white bread dough around a mixture of almond paste and candied fruits.

When making white bread, reserve half the dough when shaping into a loaf after the first rising.

Beat $\frac{3}{4}$ cup prepared almond paste with the juice of $\frac{1}{2}$ lemon and enough water to make a fairly soft mixture. Beat in $\frac{1}{2}$ cup mixed red and green candied cherries, chopped, and $\frac{1}{4}$ cup raisins.

Pat or roll the dough to an oval about $\frac{3}{4}$ inch thick and spread the filling along one side. Roll the dough around it and set on a greased baking sheet, seam side down.

Score the top of the dough with a knife in a lattice pattern, brush it with 1 egg white, beaten until frothy, and sprinkle generously with sugar. Bake in a hot oven (400°F) for 40 minutes or until the bread sounds hollow when tapped. Cool on a wire rack.

Dark Rye Bread

4 cups rye flour
4 cups wholewheat flour, preferably stone-ground
2 packages dry or 2 cakes compressed yeast
3 cups milk
1 tablespoon salt
3 tablespoons honey
3 tablespoons oil

Method

Scald the milk and let cool to lukewarm. Sprinkle the yeast over the milk and leave 5 minutes or until dissolved.

Mix the flours together with the salt and warm them in a large bowl. Make a well in the center, put in the honey and oil and pour on the milk and yeast mixture. Mix in enough flour with your hand to make a thick batter and sprinkle the top thoroughly with flour from the sides. Cover with a damp cloth and let rise in a warm place for 15–20 minutes or until bubbles break through the surface.

Mix to a dough with your hand, turn out onto a floured board and knead until stiff but pliable, working in more wholewheat flour as necessary. Grease the bowl, put back the dough, cover with the cloth and let rise again in a warm place for 2 hours or until doubled in bulk.

Set oven at moderately hot (375°F).

Turn the dough out onto a floured board and knead lightly to knock out air. Halve the dough and shape into 2 round or long loaves. Place them on a greased baking sheet, cover with the cloth and let rise again in a warm place for 30 minutes or until almost doubled in bulk.

Bake in heated oven for 50–60 minutes or until the bread sounds hollow when tapped. Cool on a wire rack.

Rye flour has less gluten than wheat flour so rye bread does not rise as high as wholewheat bread. Be sure the flour and milk are warm before mixing. For a variation of flavor, try adding 1 tablespoon grated orange rind or caraway seeds or 1 teaspoon aniseed to the flour.

French Bread

4 cups flour
$\frac{1}{2}$ cup milk
1 cup water
1 package dry or 1 cake compressed yeast
$\frac{1}{4}$ cup warm water
$1\frac{1}{2}$ teaspoons shortening
$1\frac{1}{2}$ tablespoons sugar
2 teaspoons salt

French bread as you find it in France is a dream long sought after by bakers here, both amateur and professional. Our flour, ovens, milk, and even our yeast are different, and only a passable imitation of the crisp French original has ever been achieved. Here is one of the best attempts. A sourdough version is on page 72.

Method

Heat milk with 1 cup water until boiling and let cool to lukewarm. Sprinkle the yeast over the $\frac{1}{4}$ cup warm water, leave 5 minutes or until dissolved and add the cooled milk with the shortening and $\frac{3}{4}$ tablespoon of the sugar.

Sift the flour into a warm bowl with the salt and remaining sugar, make a well in the center and pour in the yeast mixture. Stir thoroughly to mix but do not knead. The dough will be soft. Cover with a damp cloth and let rise in a warm place for 2 hours or until doubled in bulk.

Set oven at hot (400°F).

Work the dough lightly and turn out onto a floured board. Cut in half and pat into two flat rectangles 12 X 9 inches. Roll up and continue rolling, tapering the dough at the ends to form a thin loaf that is 15 inches long. Place the loaves on a greased baking sheet and cut diagonal shallow slits $\frac{1}{4}$ inch deep across the tops. Cover and let rise again in a warm place for 15–20 minutes or until almost doubled in bulk.

Bake loaves in heated oven with a pan of hot water placed in the bottom of the oven. (The steam from the pan of water ensures a crisp crust.) After 15 minutes, reduce the heat to 350°F and bake 30 minutes longer or until the loaves are crisp and brown. Cool on a wire rack.

Baps

4 cups flour
1 teaspoon salt
1½ cups mixed milk and water
¼ cup butter or shortening
1 package dry or 1 cake
   compressed yeast
1 teaspoon sugar

Baps are a Scottish specialty – light rolls with a floury, pale gold crust. They are good for breakfast, buttered and spread with jam or honey, or served plain with dinner.

Method
Sift the flour with the salt into a warm bowl. Warm the milk and water mixture, add the butter or shortening and stir until dissolved. Gently stir the compressed yeast with the sugar until creamy or dissolve the dry yeast in a little of the milk. Add the remaining lukewarm milk to the yeast with the sugar, if not already added.

Make a well in the center of the flour and pour in the yeast mixture. Mix to a soft dough, turn out onto a floured board and knead until smooth and elastic. Put the dough into a greased bowl, cover with a damp cloth and let rise in a warm place for 1–1½ hours or until doubled in bulk.

Set oven at hot (425°F).

Knead the dough lightly on a floured board and divide into 6 pieces. Roll each piece on the board to an oval or flatten with the heel of the hand. Set the rounds on a floured baking sheet, sprinkle with flour and let rise again in a warm place for 5–10 minutes or until almost doubled in bulk. Bake in heated oven for 5 minutes, lower heat to 400°F and bake 5–10 minutes longer or until the baps are pale gold. Cool on a wire rack.

Sally Lunn loaf is sliced into 3 rounds and toasted under broiler; butter each side before reshaping as a loaf to serve

Sally Lunn

4 cups flour
1½ cups milk
2 tablespoons butter
½ teaspoon salt
1 package dry or 1 cake
   compressed yeast
1 teaspoon sugar
1 egg
1 tablespoon sugar, dissolved
   in 1 tablespoon milk (for
   glaze)

8 inch springform pan

Method
Warm and grease the pan.

Warm the milk, stir in the butter until melted and let cool to lukewarm. Sift the flour and salt into a warm bowl. Stir the compressed yeast gently with the sugar until creamy or dissolve the dry yeast in a little of the warmed milk. Stir the egg into the remaining milk and add this to the yeast together with the sugar, if not already added.

Make a well in the flour and pour in the yeast mixture. Mix to a soft dough, turn out onto a floured board and knead lightly for 2–3 minutes. Shape the dough into a round and put into the warmed pan. Set oven at hot (425°F).

Cover the dough with a damp cloth and set in a warm place to rise until doubled in bulk – about 30 minutes. Bake in heated oven for 30–35 minutes or until the loaf sounds hollow when tapped. Brush the top with sweetened milk and put the loaf back in the oven for 1–2 minutes to dry the glaze. Cool on a wire rack.

Cracked Wheat Bread

1¼ cups finely cracked wheat
4 cups flour
2 teaspoons salt
2 packages dry or 2 cakes
   compressed yeast
3 cups lukewarm water

*2 medium loaf pans
(8½ X 4½ X 2½ inches)*

Cracked wheat or bulgur is whole grains of wheat milled to varying degrees of coarse-ness. It is used in Greek and Middle Eastern cooking to make pilaf and occasionally added to bread. This coarsely grained, chewy bread is quick to make as it only rises once.

Method
Grease the loaf pans.

Mix the flour and cracked wheat in a warm bowl with the salt. Sprinkle the yeast over ½ cup of the water and leave 5 minutes or until dissolved.

Make a well in the center of the flour, pour in the yeast mixture with the remaining water and mix with your hand to a dough – it should be sticky. Knead the dough lightly, then divide it in half and put into the prepared pans, smoothing the top. Cover the dough with a damp cloth and let rise in a warm place for 45 minutes or until doubled in bulk. Set oven at moderately hot (375°F).

Bake the bread in heated oven for 40 minutes or until it sounds hollow when tapped. Cool on a wire rack.

The name **Sally Lunn** is said to originate from the late 18th century, when Sally became famous for the homemade cookies that she sold in the streets of the fashionable English spa, Bath. In England today, a Sally Lunn is a typical sweet bread eaten with afternoon tea.

Breads to make at home (from left): a rich coffeecake, baps or Sally Lunn

Sourdough Bread

5 cups flour
½ cup milk
1 cup water
2 tablespoons oil
3 tablespoons sugar
2½ teaspoons salt
1 package dry or 1 cake
  compressed yeast
1⅓ cups sourdough starter
1 egg white, mixed with
  1 tablespoon cold water
  (for glaze) – optional

Makes 3 loaves, each about 12–14 inches long.

Method
Heat the milk, half the water and oil together until boiling. Remove from heat and let cool to lukewarm. Stir in the sugar and salt. Sprinkle the yeast over the remaining ½ cup water, heated to lukewarm, and leave 5 minutes or until dissolved.

Sift the flour into a large bowl, make a well in the center and pour in the lukewarm milk mixture, the dissolved yeast and the sourdough starter. Mix well with your hands, cover with a damp cloth and let stand in a warm place for 2 hours or until doubled in bulk.

Turn the dough out onto a floured board and knead until it is just smooth. Divide it into 3 parts, roll each part into a long narrow roll and cut several diagonal shallow slits on top. Place them on a greased baking sheet, cover with a cloth and let rise 30 minutes or until almost doubled in bulk.

Bake the bread in a moderately hot oven (375°F) for 45 minutes or until the bread sounds hollow when tapped. If you like, for a crisp crust, glaze the loaves by brushing them with egg white mixture about 5 minutes before removing them from the oven. A crisp crust is also obtained by placing a pan of hot water at bottom of oven so the dough is baked in steam. Cool on wire racks.

Sourdough Starter

Sourdough bread is famous for its nutty, sour flavor but notorious for being hard to make. This reputation is somewhat unjustified because sourdough bread is kneaded, left to rise and baked exactly like regular bread. The only difference is in the leavening agent – sourdough bread uses a 'starter' (a mixture of flour, sugar and milk that is left to ferment before using) as well as yeast.

Method
Put 1 cup flour into a 1 quart jar, make a well in the center and add ¼ cup sugar and 1 cup milk. Stir until mixed, cover and let stand at room temperature for at least 2 days. Starter has an acid smell and small bubbles burst through the surface when it is ready to use. At this point, the starter can be stored, covered, in the refrigerator, but bring it back to room temperature before using.

When you need more starter (but still have several tablespoons left) you can 'feed' it by adding the same amount of ingredients you used to make the original starter to these few tablespoons left in the jar. Mix and let stand at room temperature for several days.

Knead the sourdough bread dough on a floured board; sourdough starter is in the jar

Divide the dough in three, shape into loaves and cut shallow diagonal slits on top

Home-baked sourdough bread is coarse-textured and has a delicious sour, nutty flavor

PRESERVES (1)

The season for early summer fruits is short, so take advantage of their abundance while you can; preserve some fruits for future months by making a selection from the following recipes for jams, jellies, pickles and relishes. Red currants, raspberries and gooseberries appear for 2–3 weeks, if at all. Peaches and nectarines last longer, but are at their peak of quality for about a month, and strawberries, although they can be bought in the depths of winter, are incomparable when freshly picked.

JAMS

Jams can be divided into two categories — regular jam and conserves. Regular jam is based on sugar and fresh fruit, boiled together until thick; jelly is similar but only the juice of fruit is used.

Conserves were more popular when the canning of fruit was unknown. Whole or sliced fruits were preserved in heavy syrup and eaten with a spoon — as they sometimes still are in Europe — rather than as a spread. A good conserve is usually more syrupy than regular jam and has a sweeter, richer flavor.

Points to remember

1 Use dry, barely ripe fruit with good color and flavor.
2 Pick over the fruit and wash or wipe it, according to the variety.
3 Cook preserves in small quantities (make several batches if you like) so the fruit is cooked as fast as possible to keep its flavor fresh.
4 Warm sugar before adding it to the boiling fruit so the temperature of the jam is not lowered (this would cause overcooking). Freshly picked soft fruits need less preliminary cooking than fruits that have not ripened naturally.
5 When the sugar is dissolved, but not before, boil briskly, stirring slowly and gently, until the jam reaches the jell point. Do not boil for too long because this darkens the color and spoils the flavor of the jam.
6 There are three ways of testing for the jell point.
The finger test. Remove the preserving kettle from the heat, put a little jam on a cold plate and cool it quickly, or drop a little jam on the bottom of an ice cube tray taken straight from the freezer. Run your index finger through the center and, if the jam is ready, it will crinkle slightly and remain in two separate portions. It will also form a firm drop on the finger.
The temperature test. You need an accurate sugar thermometer. Warm the thermometer in hot water before use; cool it in warm water after use (to prevent it from breaking because of extreme changes in temperature). When hot, stir the jam thoroughly to make the temperature even throughout. Put warmed thermometer well into the jam; when the temperature reaches 220°F, the jell will be good. Occasionally a temperature 1–2 degrees higher produces a better result.
The sheeting test. Dip a clean wooden spoon into the jam, remove it and twirl it around until the jam on it has cooled slightly. Tilt the spoon to let jam drop from it; if this has been boiled sufficiently, the jam will partially set on the spoon and drops will run together and 'sheet', falling cleanly and sharply. This is known as the 'sheeting' stage.
7 Skim the frothy scum, if necessary, towards the end of cooking only. Continuous skimming is unnecessary and wasteful.
8 The heatproof glasses or jars for the jam must be sterilized with boiling water and dry; warm them in a very low oven before filling. Stand on a wooden board to prevent them from cracking and fill them quite full to allow for any shrinkage. If using whole fruit, such as strawberries or cherries, let the jam stand in the pan for 20–30 minutes, then stir and pour into the glasses; otherwise fruit floats to the top of the glasses.
9 Wipe the outside of the filled glasses carefully with a cloth wrung out in hot water. While jam is still very hot, or when completely cool, cover with a thin layer of melted paraffin. Jams with pectin added should always be sealed when hot. When paraffin solidifies, add a second layer and cover the glasses with their lids or circles of white or wax paper, fastened with elastic bands or string. Label each glass with the name of the jam and the date. Store in a cool, dry place.

Causes of Failure

Jam may not keep well because:
1 Mold may be caused by using wet, cold glasses; covering them when jam is neither hot nor completely cold in temperature; using insufficient paraffin, or by storing the jam in a damp place.
2 Crystallization may be caused by using too much sugar; allowing the jam to boil before all the sugar has dissolved; stirring too much when boiling, or by leaving the jam uncovered for too long.
3 Fermentation may be caused by insufficient boiling; using too little sugar, or by storing in too warm a place.

Pectin is a natural, gum-like substance in fruit that causes jellies and jams to jell. If fruit with a very low pectin content is used, it is advisable to add one of the following to ensure a proper jell: commercially prepared pectin; the acid juice of gooseberries, apples or red currants; or tartaric or citric acid, either in the form of powder dissolved in a little water, or as lemon juice.

If using commercial pectin, follow the package directions.

Apples, blackberries, cranberries, red currants, gooseberries, grapefruit, lemons, oranges and plums are generally rich in pectin, while apricots, cherries, grapes, raspberries, peaches, pineapples, strawberries and all overripe fruits tend to have a low pectin content.

To test for pectin: mix 1 tablespoon cooked unsweetened juice from the fruit with 1 tablespoon grain alcohol. Juice rich in pectin forms a large clot; juice moderately rich in pectin forms a few small clots; juice low in pectin forms a small flaky sediment.

Equipment for making Jam or Jelly

Preserving kettle. The kettle used for preserving is of prime importance. It may be enameled or made of aluminum or copper. Copper kettles should be lined with tin so that both jams and pickles can be cooked in them (the vinegar used in pickling produces an undesirable chemical from unlined copper).

Proper preserving kettles are large, about 1 foot deep with a big handle for lifting and, sometimes, a spout for pouring. A large shallow pan or flameproof casserole can be used instead of a preserving kettle for small batches of jam or jelly.

Jelly glasses. Glasses for jams and jellies are available with screw top or other metal lids in various sizes. Otherwise any glass jar will do, with or without a lid.

Funnel. A 4–5 inch diameter funnel with a wide tube is very useful for filling the jam or jelly into the glasses. It prevents stickiness on the outside of the glasses and lessens the danger of burning yourself.

Spoons. If you make jams and jellies frequently, keep several large wooden spoons specifically for this purpose. Jam spoons have a wide bowl and come in different sizes; some have a notch in the handle to catch on the side of the preserving pan so the spoon does not slide into the jam.

Paraffin. This is available in hardware stores and in most large supermarkets. It should be melted over a very low heat or over hot water. If the temperature is too hot, the paraffin will shrink away from the sides of the jelly glasses once it has solidified.

The easiest way to pour it is from a pitcher, pouring just enough to cover the jam or jelly with a thin layer. When this solidifies, cover with a second layer of paraffin, tilting the glass back and forth.

Both coatings together should measure not more than one-eighth inch in thickness. A coating that is too thick is unattractive and wasteful, but more serious than that, it frequently pulls away from the sides of the glass.

Jelly bag. For jelly-making use a jelly bag and stand or a large piece of clean linen or cotton for straining the fruit. If no stand is available, you can improvise with 2 chair backs or an upturned stool. For clear, sparkling jelly do not squeeze the bag.

Sugar. Use regular granulated sugar, made from cane or beets, for preserving.

Strawberry Jam 1

2 quarts strawberries
6 cups sugar
juice of 1 lemon
1 tablespoon unsalted butter

Method
Pick over and hull the strawberries. Crush $\frac{1}{2}$ cup berries with a fork and put in the bottom of a preserving kettle with 1 tablespoon of the sugar. Melt the sugar over gentle heat, then add the remaining fruit and bring to a boil, stirring occasionally. Heat the sugar in a low oven (250°F).

Add the warmed sugar to the pan with the strained lemon juice and boil rapidly until the jam gives a jell test. Take from heat and stir in the butter. Pour into hot, dry glasses. Cover and seal when cool.

Strawberry Jam 2

$1\frac{1}{2}$ quarts strawberries
5 cups sugar
2 cups water
a few cloves (optional)

Sugar thermometer

This is a particularly good recipe for strawberry jam, with whole berries suspended in a clear shiny jelly. For guaranteed success, cook in a wide, shallow pan and test with a sugar thermometer.

Method
Heat the sugar slowly in the water, using a preserving kettle if possible. When completely dissolved, insert a sugar thermometer, boil rapidly to the soft ball stage (234°F–238°F).

Add the fruit, cover pan and remove from heat. Let strawberries soak in the syrup for 15–20 minutes. Return to heat and bring rapidly to a boil until the syrup boils up over the fruit. Take the kettle from heat and let the syrup subside. Skim if necessary.

Repeat this process (bringing to a boil, removing from heat and skimming) twice more, then remove the strawberries with a slotted spoon. Spread them in a single layer on a fine rack with a tray beneath to catch the syrup. Return this to the syrup remaining in the kettle and reduce by rapid boiling until a drop will give a jell test.

Return the strawberries to the syrup and boil 5 minutes. If you like, tie a few cloves in a piece of cheesecloth and leave to bubble in the syrup at this stage.

Discard the cloves, if used, and pour the jam into hot, dry glasses. Cover and seal when cool.

Sun-cooked Strawberry Jam

4–5 quarts strawberries
4 cups sugar per quart of prepared strawberries

Method
Wash, drain thoroughly and hull the strawberries. Cut large berries into quarters, the small ones in half. Measure the fruit and place in a large preserving kettle. Warm 4 cups sugar for each quart of fruit in a low oven (250°F). Add to the fruit and stir gently over low heat until all the berries are coated with the dissolved sugar.

Bring to a rolling boil and boil for **exactly 3 minutes.** Pour jam immediately into flat glass, enamel, or china trays to a depth of $\frac{1}{2}$ inch. The fruit should lie flat in the syrup. Cover completely with sheets of glass and place outdoors in unobstructed sunshine. Turn the glass covers each time enough condensation accumulates inside the glass to pour off (this may be every few minutes for 1–2 hours, with longer intervals after that).

Stir the jam occasionally to expose all surfaces of the berries and syrup to the sun. Strawberries are 'cooked' when the syrup forms jelled ridges or waves when the container is tilted at one end. This usually takes about $1\frac{1}{2}$ days of full sunshine. Pour into clean dry glasses. Cover and seal.

Raspberry jam is one of the simplest jams to make

◄*Carefully add the warmed sugar to the preserving kettle of hot raspberries*

When the jam gives a jell test, ▶ *pour it into warm dry jelly glasses*

When the paraffin is solid, cover with white or wax paper ▶

Raspberry Jam

2 quarts dry raspberries
6 cups sugar

This is a particularly delicious, fresh-tasting jam.

Method
Put the fruit in a preserving kettle and set over low heat to draw out the juice. Heat the sugar in a low oven (250°F).

Add the warmed sugar carefully to the fruit and dissolve slowly, stirring occasionally. When the sugar is completely dissolved, bring the jam rapidly to boiling point, draw aside and pour into hot, dry glasses. Cover and seal when cool.

Watchpoint: be sure the jam actually boils; stir 2–3 times just before it boils to spread the heat; test with a sugar thermometer if possible — it should reach 222°F.

Blueberry Jam

2 quarts blueberries
½ cup water
5 cups sugar

Made with unripe, red blueberries, the flavor is reminiscent of Scandinavian lingonberries.

Method
Wash and pick over the blueberries. Put them in a preserving kettle with the water and simmer over moderate heat for 20 minutes or until just tender. Heat the sugar in a low oven (250°F).

Add warmed sugar and stir occasionally until mixture boils. Boil rapidly until the jam gives a jell test and pour into hot, dry glasses. Cover and seal when cool.

Gooseberry Jam

2 quarts gooseberries
2 cups water
8 cups sugar

Method
Wash, top and tail the gooseberries. Place them in a preserving kettle with the water and cook gently for 20 minutes or until soft and mushy. Heat the sugar in a low oven (250°F).

Add the warmed sugar, dissolve slowly, stirring, and then boil rapidly until the jam gives a jell test. Skim the jam and pour into hot, dry glasses. Cover and seal when cool.

Bing Cherry Jam

4 lb Bing cherries
¾ cup water
1 teaspoon tartaric acid, or
    1 cup red currant juice —
    crushed from about 1 pint
    red currants
6 cups sugar

Method
Pit the fruit and tie the pits in a piece of cheesecloth. Put the fruit in a preserving kettle with the water and the pits. Simmer gently for 15 minutes or until the cherries are tender. Heat the sugar in a low oven (250°F).

Add tartaric acid or red currant juice, followed by the warmed sugar and stir until dissolved. Boil rapidly until the jam gives a jell test. Remove the bag of pits and pour the jam into hot, dry glasses. Cover and seal when cool.

Pineapple Apricot Jam

1 lb dried apricots
1 ripe pineapple, pared and
    cored
1 quart water
¾ cup sugar per cup prepared
    fruit
20 Maraschino cherries, halved

Method
Soak apricots in the water for 1 hour or until tender. Drain apricots, reserving all the liquid and work with pineapple through the fine blade of a grinder. Stir the liquid into the purée, measure the mixture and bring to a boil in a preserving kettle. Heat the sugar in a low oven (250°F).

Add warmed sugar and cook over low heat, stirring constantly, until the sugar is dissolved. Add the cherries and bring to a boil. Simmer, stirring occasionally, until the jam is thick and gives a jell test. Pour into hot, dry glasses. Cover and seal when cool.

Spiced Cherry Preserves with Orange

4 lb Bing or dark cherries
4 juice oranges
2 sticks of cinnamon
6 cloves
½ cup lemon juice, or
    1 teaspoon tartaric acid
7 cups sugar

Method
Slice the oranges thinly, but do not peel; put them in a preserving kettle with water to cover by about ¼ inch. Add spices, tied in cheesecloth, and simmer 12–15 minutes or until the oranges are very tender. Remove spice bag.

Pit the cherries, crack a few of the pits and blanch their kernels. Add these and the cherries to the oranges with the lemon juice or tartaric acid and bring to a boil. Heat the sugar in a low oven (250°F) and add to the pan. Stir the jam until the sugar has dissolved. Boil rapidly until the jam is thick and gives a jell test. Pour into hot, dry glasses. Cover and seal when cool.

Peach Preserves

8 peaches (about 2 lb)
2 cups sugar
juice of 2 lemons, strained

Method
Take peaches, peel, cut in half and remove the pits. Put peaches in a preserving kettle and cook over a low heat, crushing them with a potato masher as they heat. Heat the sugar in a low oven (250°F).

When preserves come to a boil, stir in the warmed sugar and lemon juice. Heat gently until the sugar is dissolved, then cook preserves rapidly for 10 minutes, stirring frequently. Reduce heat to very low and cook 5 minutes longer or until the preserves give a jell test. Pour into hot, dry glasses. Cover and seal when cool.

Spiced Fig Conserve

5 lb fresh figs
1 lemon, thinly sliced
4 sticks of cinnamon, about
    2 inches long
2 teaspoons whole allspice
2 pieces of dried ginger root,
    about 1 inch long

Method
Wash the figs, cover with boiling water and let stand 1 minute. Drain the figs, rinse in cold water and peel off the skins.

In a large preserving kettle combine the figs, lemon and the spices tied in a cheesecloth bag. Bring the mixture slowly to a boil. Meanwhile heat the sugar in a low oven (250°F).

Add the warmed sugar to the fig mixture and continue cooking over a low heat until the conserve is thick and gives a jell test. Stir frequently. Remove the spice bag before spooning conserve into hot, dry glasses. Cover and seal when cool.

Blackberry and Apple Jam

2 quarts blackberries
1½ lb tart apples, pared and
    cored
rind and juice of 2 large lemons
2 cups water
10 cups sugar

Method
Slice the apples and tie the cores and the peel with lemon rind in a piece of cheesecloth. Put this bag with the sliced apples, blackberries and water into a preserving kettle and simmer until soft and pulpy. Remove cheesecloth bag. Meanwhile, heat the sugar in

a low oven (250°F).

Add strained lemon juice with the sugar and stir until dissolved. Bring to a boil and boil rapidly until the jam gives a jell test. Pour into hot, dry glasses. Cover and seal when cool.

Melon and Ginger Jam

3 large firm Persian, Crenshaw
    or honeydew melons
8 cups sugar
rind and juice of 4 lemons
¾ cup chopped candied ginger
1 cup chopped walnuts

Method
Cut the melon into large cubes, removing the peel and seeds. Put the cubes in a bowl in layers with the sugar, cover and leave 24 hours. Cut the lemon rind into needle-like strips and put into a preserving kettle with the lemon juice, ginger and melon. Bring slowly to a boil, stirring occasionally, and boil until it gives a jell test, adding walnuts towards the end of cooking. Pour into hot, dry glasses. Cover and seal when cool.

Rhubarb and Orange Jam

3 lb rhubarb, weighed after
    removing leaves and bottom
    of stalks
1 sweet orange
4½ cups sugar

Method
Wipe the rhubarb, cut it in small pieces and arrange in a bowl in layers with the sugar; cover and let stand 12 hours. Cover the orange with water and boil whole

for $1\frac{1}{2}$ hours or until it is tender; drain, and cut in quarters, discarding the seeds.

Finely slice the orange quarters and put them in a preserving kettle with the rhubarb and sugar. Bring slowly to a boil, stirring occasionally, and boil rapidly until the jam gives a jell test. Pour into hot, dry glasses. Cover and seal when cool.

JELLIES

Only the juice of the fruit is used for making jellies. The best fruits are those with a sharp natural flavor such as crab apples, plums, damson plums, raspberries and red and black currants. Tart apples and windfalls in particular are also excellent for jelly-making, especially when a second ingredient — fruit or herb — is added for more flavor and color.

Points to remember

1 Fruit jells better if underripe. It must never be overripe.
2 Jelling depends on the amount of pectin and acid in the fruit; sweet apples, for example, contain plenty of pectin, but must have lemon juice added before they will jell.

To test for acid, taste the juice; if it is sweet, add lemon or lime juice. Juice that is moderately rich in pectin may need more pectin added before it will set properly. Juice low in pectin should not be used for jelly. (See page 76 for note on pectin and how to test for jell.)
3 Soft fruits like blackberries

and red currants only need to be washed in a colander and drained; it is not necessary to remove the stalks as the liquid will be strained later.

For soft fruits (except blackberries) the juice is extracted without adding water. Place the fruit in a heatproof glass bowl or stoneware crock, crush lightly with a wooden spoon and cover with a plate. Stand the bowl or crock in a water bath and simmer gently or cook in a very low oven (250°F) until all the juice has been extracted. For a small quantity of fruit, use a double boiler.
4 Hard fruits should be washed, wiped and, if very large, cut into smaller pieces. Do not remove the peel or cores as these are valuable sources of pectin and improve the jelling quality of the fruit.
5 To keep the jelly clear and sparkling, do not try to speed up the draining process by forcing juice through the bag or cloth; this makes the jelly cloudy and unattractive.
6 Test jelly for setting like jam on a plate, with a sugar thermometer, or by the 'sheeting' method.
7 For cooking and storing jellies, follow the directions for making jam (see page 76).

To test for the jell point, run a finger through the cooled jelly; if ready it will crinkle and remain separated

Drain the blackberry juice from the pulp using a jelly bag

Blackberry Jelly

2 quarts blackberries
$\frac{3}{4}$ cup sugar per cup juice

Method

Wash the blackberries, remove the stems and crush with a potato masher. If they are very juicy, water is not needed. Should they seem dry, add $\frac{1}{4}-\frac{1}{2}$ cup water for each cup of berries.

In a preserving kettle bring the berries to a boil, reduce heat and simmer 15 minutes. Drain through a clean cloth or a jelly bag and leave to drip overnight.

Measure the juice and heat the appropriate amount of sugar in a low oven (250°F). Heat the juice, add the warmed sugar and dissolve it over gentle heat.

Boil mixture rapidly, without stirring or skimming, until it gives a jell test. Pour into hot, dry glasses. Cover and seal when cool.

Red Currant Jelly

2 quarts red currants
$\frac{3}{4}$ cup sugar per cup juice

Method

Wash fruit and, without removing the stems, put in a large heatproof glass jar or stone crock. Cover and stand in a deep pan of hot water. Simmer on top of the stove or in a very low oven (250°F) for 1 hour or until all the juice is extracted, mashing the fruit from time to time with a potato masher.

Ladle the fruit into a clean cloth or jelly bag and let drip overnight. Measure juice into preserving kettle and heat the appropriate amount of sugar in a low oven (250°F). Heat the juice, add the warmed sugar and continue heating gently, stirring, until sugar is dissolved.

Bring to a boil, boil vigorously for 3–5 minutes, skim with a metal spoon and continue boiling if necessary until it gives a jell test. When ready, pour jelly into hot, dry glasses. Cover and seal when cool.

Apple Jelly

6 lb tart apples or crab apples
7 cups water
¾ cup sugar, warmed, for every
   1 cup juice
2–3 strips of lemon rind

Method
Wash apples, wipe and cut into pieces (crab apples may be left whole), removing any bruised parts. Put fruit into a preserving kettle with the water and simmer until very soft, stirring and crushing occasionally. Ladle this pulp into a clean, dry cloth or a jelly bag to drip overnight.

Measure juice and add sugar in correct proportion. Return juice to pan and stir over heat until sugar has completely dissolved. Add lemon rind to kettle; boil rapidly until it gives a jell test. Remove lemon rind and pour jelly into hot, dry glasses. Cover and seal when cool.

Rose Geranium Jelly

Make apple jelly with crab or tart apples. When the sugar has dissolved in the juice, add 3–4 rose geranium leaves, tied together; continue to boil. Remove the leaves when the jelly is well flavored; cook until it gives a jell test. Pour into hot, dry glasses. Cover and seal when cool.

Lemon Verbena Jelly

Make as for rose geranium jelly, but use tart apples; add a handful of lemon verbena leaves tied in cheesecloth.

PICKLES & RELISHES

Points to remember

1 In cooking, use heatproof glass, enamel, stainless steel or tinned copper containers; vinegar attacks metals like aluminum and the pickles will be discolored with a harsh flavor. Pack pickles in jars, preferably with glass tops to avoid corrosion.
2 Use only firm, unbruised fruits and vegetables; they can be slightly underripe.
3 Cut ingredients into even-sized pieces so they pickle evenly.
4 Pickling salt gives better results than iodized table salt, particularly for pickles pre-served in brine. Cider vinegar is a good choice for pickles as its flavor is pleasantly mellow. White distilled vinegar is used to keep the color of light-colored vegetables like onions.
5 Taste the pickles before sealing as the amount of salt and sugar needed can vary with the ingredients.
6 Be sure pickles are completely immersed in liquid to avoid deterioration.
7 If pickling in a crock in brine, skim the scum from the surface regularly.
8 Make sure both jars and tops are sterilized and dry before spooning in the hot pickle and sealing at once with the rubber ring and metal clamp. Rubber rings must be fresh for each batch of pickles, although the jars can be used again. When properly sealed, the pickles will keep for several weeks (see individual recipes).

Some of the many fruits and vegetables good for preserving as pickles and relishes

Spiced Nectarines

3 lb nectarines
2½ cups distilled vinegar
12–18 cloves
two 3 inch pieces of
   cinnamon stick
8 allspice berries
4 cups sugar

Method
Bring vinegar and spices, tied together in cheesecloth, to a boil in a large shallow pan. Add sugar and dissolve slowly without boiling.

Pour boiling water over the nectarines, let stand 15 seconds, drain and peel them. Cut in half, twist gently and remove the pits. Bring vinegar mixture to a boil and add nectarines, rounded side down. Simmer until very tender.
Watchpoint: allow 15–20 minutes for the nectarines to cook so the flavor of the vinegar and spices penetrates the fruit; this also prevents any discoloration after the fruit has been packed in jars.

Lift the fruit out of the pan with a slotted spoon and pack in hot, dry jars. Boil the liquid hard for 3 minutes or until syrupy, remove the spice bag before pouring the liquid over the nectarines in the jars. Seal at once. Keeps 3–4 weeks.

Spiced Peaches and Apricots

Spice peaches and apricots in the same way as nectarines but leave apricots whole if they are small.

Spiced Cherries

4 lb Bing cherries
4 cups sugar
2½ cups cider vinegar
3 walnut-sized pieces of root
   ginger, sliced
1 stick of cinnamon
3–4 cloves
peeled rind of ½ lemon

Method
Pit the cherries, put in a glass bowl or crock and stand this in a deep water bath. Heat gently on top of stove or in a low oven (250°F) for 30 minutes or until cherries are barely tender.

Meanwhile heat the sugar in vinegar until dissolved, bring to a boil and add the ginger, spices and lemon rind, tied in cheesecloth bag. Simmer 10 minutes.

Pack the cherries in hot, dry glass jars and add their juice to the pickling liquid in the pan. Remove spices in the cheesecloth; boil hard to produce a thick syrup. Pour this over the cherries and seal at once. Keeps 3–4 weeks in the refrigerator.

Spiced Oranges

5 large sweet oranges
1¼ cups white wine vinegar
2½ cups sugar
2 inch stick of cinnamon
7 whole cloves
3 blades of mace

This is a good accompaniment to cold meats, especially ham. Pack into large glasses or jars, preferably 2 lb or more, so the flavor mellows well, and keep at least 2 weeks before eating.

Method
Cut the oranges in ¼ inch slices, removing the seeds,

Stuff and pickle peaches with chopped onion, sweet pepper, walnuts and cinnamon before simmering with white vinegar, sugar and cloves

and put them in a pan with water just to cover. Put the lid half on the pan and simmer the oranges for 20 minutes or until the peel is tender.

Put the vinegar, sugar and spices, tied in cheesecloth, in a preserving kettle and boil 5 minutes. Drain the oranges, reserving the cooking liquid, and put about half the slices into the syrup; simmer gently for about 30 minutes.

Watchpoint: it is most important that the slices are completely covered by liquid, so it is easiest to cook them in two batches.

Lift out the cooked slices with a slotted spoon into a bowl. Add remaining orange slices to the pan and, if not covered by syrup, add a little of the reserved cooking liquid. Simmer as before, then add the syrup and orange slices to those already cooked, cover and leave overnight.

In the morning, drain off the syrup, bring to a boil until thick and add the orange slices. Or, if the syrup is already thick, simply heat it slowly to boiling point with the orange slices. Pour into hot, dry glasses or jars and seal at once.

Stuffed Pickled Peaches

10 freestone peaches
1 medium onion,
   finely chopped
2 teaspoons finely chopped
   red bell pepper
3 tablespoons chopped
   walnuts
2 teaspoons cinnamon
5 cups sugar
1½ cups water
1 cup white vinegar
12 cloves

Method
Pour the boiling water over the peaches, leave 10 seconds, drain and peel them. With a small pointed knife cut around the stem end of each peach and gently loosen the pit. Remove it from the peach as neatly as possible. Combine the onion, red pepper, walnuts and cinnamon and stuff the mixture into the peach cavities.

In a preserving kettle combine the sugar, water, vinegar and cloves, tied in a cheesecloth bag, and bring to a boil. Add the peaches and simmer 15–20 minutes or until they are cooked through but still hold their shape.

Watchpoint: cook peaches very gently but thoroughly so spiced vinegar penetrates fruit and prevents discoloration.

Remove the cloves and pack the peaches into hot, and dry wide-necked jars. Fill jars almost to the top with the boiling liquid and seal at once. Keeps 3–4 weeks.

Cantaloupe Pickle

3 large cantaloupe melons
2 cups water
2 cups vinegar
3½ cups sugar
pinch of salt
¼ teaspoon oil of cinnamon
½ teaspoon oil of cloves

Oil of cinnamon and oil of cloves are available at most pharmacies.

Method

Remove the seeds and peel from the melons, then cut the flesh into cubes. Place cubes in a bowl or crock.

Combine the water, vinegar, sugar, salt, oil of both cinnamon and cloves and bring to a boil in a preserving kettle. Pour the hot liquid over melon cubes and let stand overnight in the refrigerator.

In the morning drain off the liquid, bring to a boil and pour again over the melon cubes. Refrigerate overnight.

Repeat this operation for two more consecutive mornings. Then heat the melon and liquid together until they boil, pour into hot, dry jars and seal at once. Keeps 2–3 weeks in the refrigerator.

Pickled Cherry Tomatoes

4 quarts firm cherry tomatoes
6 cups sugar
2 cups cider vinegar
2 cups water
3 walnut-sized pieces of fresh ginger root, grated
grated rind and juice of 2 lemons
1 teaspoon salt

Method

Hull and wash tomatoes and prick each in several places with a needle. Heat the sugar in the vinegar and water in a preserving kettle until dissolved, bring to a boil and boil rapidly for 5 minutes. Add tomatoes and cook 10 minutes, or until they are just tender. Remove tomatoes with a slotted spoon and add ginger, lemon rind and juice and salt. Simmer syrup 15 minutes, return tomatoes to the pan and cook 20 minutes longer or until thick and tomatoes look transparent.

Pack tomatoes in hot, dry jars, pour over the syrup and seal at once. Keeps 2–3 weeks in the refrigerator.

Spiced Prunes with Cranberry Relish

1 lb prunes
2 cups cranberries
1½ cups red Burgundy wine
5 peppercorns
3 cardamom seeds
¼ teaspoon allspice
¼ teaspoon nutmeg
1 stick of cinnamon
1 orange
½ cup sugar

Serve as a garnish with roast lamb, pork or duck.

Method

Cook the prunes with the wine and all the spices in a covered preserving kettle over very low heat until tender when tested with a fork. While the prunes are cooking, cut the orange, including the skin but discarding the seeds, and put through a food chopper with the cranberries. Stir in sugar and let stand for ½ hour.

When the prunes are tender, drain, remove the pits and fill the cavities with the relish. Keep covered in refrigerator for up to 1 week.

Spiced Crab Apples

4 lb crab apples
4½ cups sugar
1 quart vinegar
2 sticks of cinnamon
½ tablespoon whole cloves

Method

Choose firm, ripe crab apples, free from blemishes. Do not pare; leave the stems attached.

In a large preserving kettle combine the sugar, vinegar, and spices, tied in a cheesecloth bag. Bring slowly to a boil, and boil for 5 minutes. Add the fruit, bring back to a boil, then reduce the heat and cook slowly until the apples are tender. Let fruit stand in the syrup overnight.

Next day, drain off the syrup and cook until it is the consistency of maple syrup. Pack the fruit in a covered container, pour syrup over it and refrigerate. Keeps well, covered, in the refrigerator for about 4–6 weeks.

Pickled Jerusalem Artichokes

2 lb Jerusalem artichokes
1 cup white vinegar
1 cup water
1 cup sugar
5 whole cloves
½ teaspoon salt

Method

Peel the artichokes and cook whole in boiling, salted water for about 15 minutes or until tender. Test with a toothpick. Do not overcook.

Drain well and pack the artichokes into hot, dry jars, adding a few cloves to each one.

Heat the remaining ingredients until the sugar dissolves and bring to a boil. Pour the mixture over the artichokes and seal at once. Keeps well in the refrigerator for 3–4 weeks.

> **Jerusalem or root artichokes** have nothing to do with Jerusalem, but instead are native to the U.S. The name is a corruption of girasole, the Italian for sunflower – Jerusalem artichoke is the root of a type of sunflower. They were discovered in Massachusetts by the explorer Champlain and he introduced them to Europe. The French named them 'Topinambours' after the Topinambour Indians who had recently paid a visit to the French court.
>
> These root artichokes, a familiar part of the diet of the early settlers, are treated like a potato in the eastern Mediterranean and eaten with everything – even as a dessert.
>
> Although rarely found in supermarkets today, Jerusalem artichokes are well worth buying.

Pickled Carrots

12–16 very small carrots, trimmed
1 cup sugar
1½ cups white vinegar
1 teaspoon whole cloves
2 sticks of cinnamon
2 bay leaves
6 peppercorns
1½ teaspoons salt
dash of Tabasco

Serve these carrots as a pickle or as part of a salad.

Method
Cook whole carrots (don't peel or scrape if carrots are really young) in boiling, salted water for 10–15 minutes or until tender when pierced with a fork. Drain.

Heat the sugar and vinegar until dissolved and bring to a boil. Tie cloves, cinnamon, bay leaves and peppercorns in cheesecloth and add to the sugar and vinegar with salt and Tabasco. Cook over very low heat for 15 minutes.

Pack carrots in hot, dry jars and pour over the hot spicy vinegar (remove spice bag), cover tightly and cool. Store in the refrigerator; they keep for about 6–8 weeks.

Beet Relish

4 lb fresh beets, cooked or 4 cans (1 lb each) beets
½ cup prepared horseradish
2 tablespoons brown sugar
2 tablespoons granulated sugar
⅓ cup cider vinegar
2 teaspoons salt

This relish is good with boiled beef and tongue.

Method
Work the cooked fresh beets or drained canned ones through the fine blade of a food chopper. Combine the beets with all the remaining ingredients, cover and let mixture mellow in the refrigerator for about 2 hours. It can be stored, covered, in refrigerator up to 8 weeks.

Pickled Beets and Eggs

2 lb fresh beets or 2 cans (1¼ lb each) beets
8 hard-cooked eggs, peeled
1 cup sugar
1 cup water, or 1 cup liquid from canned beets
¾ cup vinegar
1½ tablespoons salt
¼ teaspoon pepper, freshly ground
2 bay leaves
10 whole cloves

Method
If fresh beets are used, leave about 2 inches of the stems attached. Cook in boiling water until tender when tested with a fork – this takes 25–45 minutes depending on age and size. Drain; cover with cold water. Slip off the skins with your fingers. If canned beets are used, drain and save liquid.

Cut the beets in slices and place in a large bowl with the hard-cooked eggs. Heat the sugar, water or beet liquid, vinegar, seasonings, bay leaves and cloves, tied in a cheesecloth bag, until the sugar dissolves and bring to a boil. Reduce heat and cook slowly for about 5 minutes.

Remove the cheesecloth bag. Pour the hot pickling liquid over the beets and eggs, cover, cool a little and chill at least 12 hours to mellow before using. Keeps, covered, in the refrigerator for about 1 week.

Green Bean Relish

1 lb fresh green beans
6 small onions
⅓ cup olive oil
juice of 1 large lemon
1 teaspoon salt
1 teaspoon sugar
pepper (to taste)
¼ teaspoon paprika

Serve with cold roasts or in salads.

Method
Trim the beans and French cut them in long thin slivers. Blanch them in boiling water for about 5 minutes (they should be quite crisp). Drain, refresh and drain them again.

Cut the onions in thin slices, add to the beans with the oil, lemon juice, salt, sugar, pepper and paprika. Toss well and chill relish in the refrigerator for several hours to develop the flavor. It can be kept, covered, in the refrigerator for 2–3 weeks.

Corn Relish

6 ears of fresh corn or 1 medium can whole kernel corn
½ green bell pepper
3 tablespoons pimiento
5 stalks of celery
1 large onion
⅔ cup olive oil
2½ tablespoons wine vinegar
2½ teaspoons salt
1 teaspoon black pepper, freshly ground
1 teaspoon dry mustard

This is a good relish for cold roasts, sandwiches, salads.

Method
Cook fresh corn in boiling unsalted water for 6–10 minutes. Slice kernels away from the cob with a sharp knife when corn is cool enough to handle. If canned corn is used, drain it thoroughly.

Finely chop green pepper (trimmed of seeds and core), pimiento, celery and onion. Add these vegetables to the corn with the oil and vinegar. Season with salt, pepper and mustard and let stand for several hours to mellow. Store, covered, in the refrigerator; it keeps up to 1 month.

Cabbage Relish

1 medium head of green cabbage
2 tablespoons salt
1 clove of garlic, crushed
2 bay leaves
12 peppercorns
3 tablespoons sugar
5 tablespoons wine vinegar

This relish is good with cold roasts, in sandwiches or in salads.

Method
Chop the cabbage into thin shreds and place in a large bowl. Mix in salt and let stand in a cool place for 24 hours, stirring occasionally. Squeeze out as much liquid as possible with your fist and return the drained cabbage to the bowl. (There should be about 4 cups cabbage.) Season with crushed garlic, bay leaves and peppercorns, tied in cheesecloth, sugar and vinegar and mix thoroughly. Let stand for several hours to pickle. Keep in refrigerator, covered, up to 12 months.

Remove cheesecloth bag before serving.

Serve Steak and Kidney Pie ~an English Specialty

Stuff eggs with cod's roe and try a hearty English steak and kidney pie. Finish with stuffed apples in meringue or tipsy cake.

Needless to say, a steak and kidney pie calls for a full-bodied wine. A good choice is Gigondas — a zestful, almost spicy red from the southern Rhône valley — or one of its neighbors from the nearby Châteauneuf-du-Pape district. As an American alternative you might consider a Zinfandel from one of the best California winemakers. Be sure to have enough of either wine to accompany the eggs à la grecque, because the cod's roe filling gives the dish a pungent flavor that is best complemented by red wine.

Eggs à la Grecque

Steak & Kidney Pie
Mashed Potatoes   Brussels Sprouts

Stuffed Apples in Meringue
with Chocolate Sauce
or
Tipsy Cake

Red wine — Gigondas (France)
or Zinfandel (California)

TIMETABLE

Day before
Hard cook the eggs; peel and keep in cold water. Make the mayonnaise and vinaigrette dressing.
Make flaky pastry dough and chill.
Poach apples, drain and stuff with dried fruit mixture.
Prepare and bake tipsy cake and store in airtight container. Make syrup for moistening the cake and cover.

Morning
Cut meat and fill the pie dish.
Scald, peel and slice tomatoes. Cover with plastic wrap and refrigerate. Make filling for eggs and store, covered, in refrigerator.
Cover pie with pastry and decorate.
Trim Brussels sprouts; peel potatoes and keep in cold water.
Prepare chocolate sauce and put in double boiler ready to reheat.
Thaw frozen raspberries for tipsy cake.
Prepare lemon garnish for tomatoes.

Assemble equipment for final cooking from 6:00 for dinner around 8 p.m.

Order of Work

6:00
Set oven at hot (425°F).
Soak tipsy cake in wine syrup.
6:15
Brush pastry with egg glaze and put pie in oven to bake.
Soak gelatin for eggs; add to mayonnaise. Drain eggs and fill; arrange on platter and coat with mayonnaise.
6:45
Reduce oven to moderately low (325°F); cover pastry with foil.
Complete egg dish.
7:15
Cook potatoes and sprouts. Turn oven to low (300°F). Make meringue and cover apples. Sprinkle with sugar and put in oven.
Whip cream and finish tipsy cake. Chill.
Drain, refresh and drain Brussels sprouts.
7:45
Drain potatoes, dry, mash with butter and cover with $\frac{1}{2}$ inch layer of hot milk. Keep warm (beat before serving). Warm Brussels sprouts with butter, shaking pan to prevent them from sticking.
8:00 Serve appetizer.
Warm chocolate sauce over low heat before serving.

You will find that **cooking times** given in the individual recipes for these dishes have sometimes been adapted in the timetable to help you when cooking and serving this menu as a party meal.

Appetizer

Eggs à la Grecque

6 hard-cooked eggs
1 jar (7$\frac{1}{2}$ oz) smoked cod's roe or any smoked fish roe
$\frac{1}{4}$ cup unsalted butter
squeeze of lemon juice
1 envelope gelatin
$\frac{1}{2}$ cup tomato juice
$\frac{1}{2}$ teaspoon paprika
3 ripe tomatoes, peeled and sliced
$\frac{1}{2}$ teaspoon sugar
vinaigrette dressing, made with $\frac{1}{4}$ cup oil, salt, freshly ground black pepper, thinly peeled rind and juice of $\frac{1}{2}$ lemon

For mayonnaise
2 egg yolks
salt and pepper
$\frac{1}{4}$–$\frac{1}{2}$ teaspoon dry mustard
$\frac{3}{4}$ cup salad oil
2 tablespoons wine vinegar

Method
To make the mayonnaise: beat the egg yolks and seasonings together with a whisk until thick. Start adding the oil, drop by drop, beating the mixture constantly. When 2 tablespoons of oil have been added and the mixture is very thick, stir in 1 teaspoon of the vinegar.

Add remaining oil a little more quickly, about 1 tablespoon at a time, and beat thoroughly until it is absorbed. If using a blender, the oil can be added in a thin stream. When all the oil is added, stir in remaining vinegar to taste with salt and pepper if needed.

Cut the eggs in half lengthwise and work the yolks through a sieve. Keep the whites in a bowl of cold water until needed.

Cream the butter in a bowl, add the roe and egg yolks and pound the mixture in a mortar and pestle, adding the lemon juice and 1–2 tablespoons mayonnaise to make the mixture a creamy consistency, or purée the mixture in a blender. Dry the egg whites on paper towels, fill with the mixture, reshape each egg and arrange on a large platter.

Sprinkle the gelatin over the tomato juice and let stand 5 minutes or until it is soft. Stand it in a pan of hot water, stir to dissolve, then stir into the mayonnaise. Cool the mixture and, when the mayonnaise begins to thicken, spoon it evenly over the eggs, using a large spoon. Sprinkle the tops with a little paprika.

Make the vinaigrette dressing. Arrange the tomato slices with the eggs on the platter, sprinkle with sugar and spoon over the dressing. Cut the lemon rind in fine shreds and blanch in boiling water for 1 minute. Drain them, pat dry on paper towels and scatter over the tomatoes.

For eggs à la grecque, pound cod's roe, yolks and butter together

Fill the egg white halves with the cod's roe and mayonnaise mixture

Reshape the egg halves and arrange on a platter

Spoon the mayonnaise over the filled eggs; spoon vinaigrette dressing over tomatoes and scatter over lemon rind

Steak and kidney pie, served with Brussels sprouts, is a hearty English dish

Entrée

Steak and Kidney Pie

$1\frac{1}{2}$ lb top round steak
$\frac{1}{2}$ lb beef kidney
2 cup quantity of flaky pastry
1 shallot or $\frac{1}{2}$ small onion, finely chopped
1 tablespoon seasoned flour, made with $\frac{1}{2}$ teaspoon salt and $\frac{1}{4}$ teaspoon pepper
1 teaspoon chopped parsley (optional)
$1\frac{1}{2}$ cups stock or cold water
additional hot stock or water (to dilute gravy)
1 egg, beaten with $\frac{1}{2}$ teaspoon salt (for glaze)

Deep 10 inch pie dish or casserole ($1\frac{1}{2}$ quart capacity); small funnel or egg cup

Method
Prepare the flaky pastry dough and chill 30 minutes. Grease the pie dish or casserole well and set the oven at hot (425°F).

Cut the steak into 1 inch cubes; remove the skin and core from the beef kidney and cut into pieces.

Arrange the funnel or egg cup in the center of the pie dish or casserole and add the meat, sprinkling each layer with shallot or onion, a little seasoned flour and chopped parsley, if used. Pour in the stock or cold water.
Watchpoint: if using stock, add less seasoning to the flour.

To cover the pie with pastry: roll out the prepared dough to $\frac{1}{4}$ inch thickness on a lightly floured marble slab or board and cut off a piece large enough to cover and slightly overlap the top of the dish. Roll out remaining dough a little thinner and cut 2 strips, each about $\frac{1}{2}$ inch wide. Dampen the edge of the pie dish with a pastry brush dipped in water and press on strips of dough. Brush them with a little cold water; cover pie with sheet of dough.
Watchpoint: do not stretch the dough when covering the pie or it will shrink during baking and slide into the dish.

When trimming the dough to fit the dish, lift the pie with one hand and, holding a knife at an angle away from the dish, cut off the overlapping dough in short, quick strokes. If it is trimmed in one continuous cut, the dragging, pulling movement prevents the pastry from rising in flakes and spoils pie's appearance.

Press down the edges of the dough to seal and scallop the edge with a knife. Use any remaining trimmings of dough to make a center decoration of leaves.

Brush the top of the pie with egg glaze, arrange the center decoration and brush again with glaze. Cut a hole in the center of dough with a knife to let steam escape.

Bake 20–30 minutes in heated oven or until the pastry is risen and brown. Then cover pie with a large sheet of foil, pleating and twisting it under the dish to hold it in place. This prevents the pastry from becoming too brown and hard during the long baking period.

Reduce oven heat to moderately low (325°F) and bake $1\frac{1}{2}$ hours longer or until the meat is tender when tested through the pastry with a skewer.

To serve: cut the first serving of pie, then pour $\frac{1}{2}$–$\frac{3}{4}$ cup hot stock or water into the pie to dilute and increase the amount of gravy. Serve with Brussels sprouts and mashed potatoes.

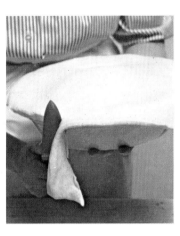

To trim excess pastry from the pie, lift dish with one hand and, holding knife at an angle away from the dish, cut in short, quick strokes

Pie funnels. The famous English steak and kidney pie is made in a deep pie dish with a rim. During cooking, the filling tends to shrink and the pastry can collapse if it is not supported in the center. In England, special pie funnels are available (but an egg cup turned upside down can be used instead).

This center funnel with its cutaway base and open top provides a natural way for steam to escape during baking and so prevents the pastry from becoming soggy underneath.

This hole is usually camouflaged with a decoration of pastry leaves or, as in England, a special china bird is inserted into the funnel before serving the pie (see photograph on page 86).

Flaky Pastry

2 cups flour
pinch of salt
6 tablespoons butter
6 tablespoons shortening or lard
8–10 tablespoons ice water

Method
Sift the flour with the salt into a bowl. Divide the fats into 4 portions (2 of butter, 2 of shortening or lard and use alternately); rub 1 portion, either butter or shortening — with the fingertips into the flour and mix with enough cold water to make a firm dough. The amount of water needed varies with different flours, but an average quantity for 2 cups flour is just over $\frac{1}{2}$ cup or 8–10 tablespoons. The more finely ground the flour, the more water it will absorb.

Knead the dough lightly until it is smooth, then roll out to a rectangle about 15 X 6 inches. Put a second portion of fat (not the same kind as the first portion rubbed in), cut in small pieces, onto two-thirds of the dough. Fold in three, put in a cloth or plastic wrap and chill 15 minutes.

Place the dough so that the open edge is towards you; roll out again to a rectangle. Put on a third portion of fat in pieces, fold the dough in three, put in a cloth or plastic wrap and refrigerate 15 minutes.

Roll out the dough again, put on the remaining fat, cut in pieces, and roll and fold as before. If dough looks streaky, roll out and fold it once more.

Dessert

Stuffed Apples in Meringue
with Chocolate Sauce

6 large Golden Delicious or any similar dessert apples
3 tablespoons sugar, dissolved in 1½ cups water
1 vanilla bean or ½ teaspoon vanilla extract

For stuffing
½ cup chopped dried mixed fruits (raisins, figs, dates, prunes, apricots)
2 tablespoons chopped candied orange or lemon peel
1 tablespoon butter

For meringue
2 egg whites
½ cup sugar
little sugar (for sprinkling)

For chocolate sauce
2 tablespoons cocoa
1 tablespoon sugar

Pastry bag and a medium star tube (optional)

Method
Bring the sugar and water mixture to a boil, add the vanilla bean, if used, and boil steadily for 10 minutes. Remove vanilla bean or, if using extract, add now.

Pare and core the apples and poach them in the syrup for about 20 minutes, turning them occasionally during cooking until they are tender when tested with a skewer but still hold their shape. Lift out the apples with a slotted spoon and transfer them to an ovenproof serving dish; reserve the syrup.

To make the stuffing: combine the dried fruits and candied peel in a saucepan with the butter and 1 tablespoon of the reserved syrup. Cook over low heat, stirring frequently, for about 5 minutes. Spoon the mixture into the apple cavities.

To make the meringue: beat the egg whites until they hold a stiff peak, add 1 tablespoon sugar and beat 1 minute until glossy. Fold in the remaining sugar carefully.

Cover each apple with meringue, preferably using a pastry bag fitted with a star tube. Sprinkle meringues with sugar and bake in a low oven (275°F–300°F) for 15–20 minutes or until golden.

To make the chocolate sauce: mix the cocoa and sugar with a little of the reserved poaching syrup until it is a paste. Stir into remaining poaching syrup and simmer 10–15 minutes or until the sauce thickens. Pour hot chocolate sauce around or over apples before serving, or serve it separately.

Just before serving, pour hot chocolate sauce over a stuffed baked apple, covered with cooked meringue

Alternative dessert

Tipsy Cake

½ cup flour
½ cup potato starch or arrowroot
pinch of salt
5 eggs (2 separated)
1¼ cups sugar
grated rind of 1 lemon

For wine syrup
1½ cups sweet white wine
½ cup sugar
6 tablespoons water
2 tablespoons brandy

To finish
2 packages frozen raspberries, thawed and well drained
Chantilly cream, made with
  1 cup heavy cream, stiffly whipped and flavored with
  1 tablespoon sugar and
  ½ teaspoon vanilla

9 inch springform pan

Method
Grease the pan and sprinkle with a mixture of sugar and flour, discarding the excess. Set oven at moderate (350°F). Sift the flour with the potato starch or arrowroot and salt.

In a bowl beat 3 whole eggs, 2 egg yolks and sugar over a pan of hot but not boiling water until the mixture is thick and leaves a ribbon trail when the beater is lifted. Take from the heat and continue beating until the mixture is cool. If using an electric beater, no heat is needed.

Beat the 2 remaining egg whites until they hold a soft shape. Using a large metal spoon fold them into the egg and sugar mixture alternately with the sifted flour mixture and grated lemon rind. Pour into prepared pan and bake

45–60 minutes in heated oven or until the cake pulls away from the sides of the pan. Turn out onto a wire rack to cool.

With a serrated-edge knife cut out a 'cone' from the center of the cake (about 5–6 inches across and 2½ inches deep). Lift out the cone.

To make the wine syrup: heat the sugar with water and boil 2 minutes. Cool and stir in the sweet wine and brandy.

To finish: pour about two-thirds of the wine syrup very gradually into the cake cavity. Fill the center with half of the Chantilly cream and half the raspberries. Replace the cone and moisten it with the remaining wine syrup. Spoon remaining cream over the top and add the rest of the raspberries.

Cut out the 'cone' of tipsy cake and moisten it with rum; fill the cavity with Chantilly cream and fruit

An English specialty

Tipsy cake, decorated with Chantilly cream and raspberries, is a luscious dessert

Hot chocolate is a delicious warming drink (recipe is on page 96)

COOKING WITH CHOCOLATE

Chocolate is unexpectedly tricky when it comes to cooking – in France to be a 'chocolatier' is a profession in itself. Chocolate goes through complicated manufacturing processes so that each kind – sweet, semisweet and unsweetened – has quite different effects in cooking; each contains different quantities of cocoa butter and melts at different temperatures, so one kind must never be substituted for another unless the recipe explains how to do it.

The easiest way to melt squares of chocolate is to cut them up or grate them and put them on a heatproof plate over a pan of hot water. When the chocolate starts to melt, work it well with a metal spatula or knife; this helps to keep the chocolate glossy. Do not let it become more than lukewarm (about 100°F) or it will look dull when it cools. When necessary, chill it in the refrigerator only until it sets because chocolate also loses its gloss when very cold.

When melting squares of chocolate in liquid, cook it very gently, stirring from time to time. If the chocolate gets too hot or if too little liquid has been added, it may suddenly stiffen and appear to separate; if this happens take it from the heat and stir in a little more cold liquid until it becomes smooth and shiny again.

The flavor of chocolate desserts mellows and improves on standing. Rich mixtures like suprême of chocolate can be kept for several days in the refrigerator, although dishes containing cream or milk should be eaten within a day or two.

Hot Chocolate

6 squares (6 oz) semisweet
  chocolate
3½ cups hot water
6 tablespoons sugar
½ cup heavy cream, whipped
  until it holds a soft shape
½ cup heavy cream, stiffly
  whipped (for serving) –
  optional

Rich, foamy hot chocolate with a really smooth texture is produced by simmering the mixture and beating or 'milling' it fairly constantly during cooking. This quantity makes 4–6 cups.

Method
Add the chocolate to 1 cup of the water. Melt it over gentle heat, bring to a boil, add the sugar and one-third of the remaining water and simmer 5–6 minutes.

Add the rest of the water and simmer until the chocolate is creamy and smooth and the consistency of custard, beating it occasionally. Pour into 4–6 cups, stir in a spoonful of lightly whipped cream and serve with extra whipped cream, if you like.

Chocolate Beaters
Special beaters are made for hot chocolate – many come from Mexico, where chocolate is a favorite drink. The beater consists of a long wooden handle with a short, ridged barrel at the end, that is made of wood or sometimes of porcelain.
To beat chocolate: twirl the handle of the beater between the palms of your hands. If you have no beater, use a flat or balloon wire whisk.

Peruvian Cream

4 squares (4 oz) semisweet
  chocolate
3 cups milk
½ cup coarsely ground coffee
½ teaspoon vanilla
½ cup sugar
2 tablespoons hot water
5 egg yolks
1 egg

For serving (optional)
½ cup heavy cream,
  whipped until it holds a
  soft shape
chocolate caraque
  (see box)

*Baking or soufflé dish
(1½ quart capacity)*

Method
Scald the milk with the ground coffee, cover and let stand to infuse for 10–15 minutes until well-flavored; strain and add vanilla.

In a small heavy-based pan cook the sugar over gentle heat, stirring occasionally, until it is a light brown caramel. Take from heat, carefully add the hot water to caramel and dissolve over gentle heat. Stir in about 2 cups of the coffee-flavored milk. Set oven at moderate (350°F).

Cut up or grate the chocolate, put it in a pan with the remaining coffee-flavored milk and melt it over low heat, stirring. When smooth, add to the caramel-flavored milk.

Beat the egg yolks and egg until well mixed, stir in the flavored milk and strain into the dish. Set in a water bath and bake in heated oven for 30–35 minutes or until a knife inserted in the center comes out clean. Chill.

Serve Peruvian cream plain or cover with a rough layer of lightly whipped cream and decorate with caraque.

Chocolate Caraque

Grate 3 squares (3 oz) semisweet chocolate and melt on a heatproof plate over a pan of hot water. Work with a metal spatula until smooth and spread thinly on a marble slab or Formica-type surface. Leave until nearly set.

Hold a sharp, long knife almost at a right angle to the surface; shave off long chocolate scrolls or flakes, using a slight sideways sawing movement. These can be kept a short time in an airtight container but caraque looks better when freshly made.

Shave off long scrolls or flakes to make chocolate caraque

Chocolate Snowball

2 bars (4 oz each) sweet
  chocolate
½ cup strong black coffee
1 cup butter
1 cup sugar
4 eggs

For decoration
1½ cups heavy cream, stiffly
  whipped
candied violets

*Charlotte mold, or deep soufflé
  dish (1 quart capacity);
  pastry bag and a star tube*

Method
Cut up the chocolate and melt it in the coffee in a saucepan over gentle heat; cook, stirring, until the mixture is thick. Add the butter and sugar, a little at a time and stir until dissolved. Heat until very hot, take from heat and beat the eggs, one at a time into the hot mixture. Set oven at moderate (350°F).

Line the mold or dish with foil and strain the chocolate mixture into it. Bake in heated oven for 25–30 minutes or until a thick crust has formed on top. Chill for at least 24 hours or up to 7 days in the refrigerator.

An hour or two before serving, run a knife around the mold and turn it out onto a platter. Peel away the foil – the mixture tends to stick and may look very messy. Put the cream into the pastry bag fitted with the star tube and cover the mold all over with rosettes of whipped cream so that no chocolate can be seen. Stud the cream haphazardly with candied violets and chill until serving. Serves 6.

Pears belle Hélène are coated with orange chocolate sauce

Orange Chocolate Sauce

1 orange
6 squares (6 oz) unsweetened chocolate
1½ cups water
½ cup sugar
pinch of salt
4 cubes of sugar

Makes about 1½ cups.

Method
Rub the sugar cubes over the orange until saturated with zest (oil).

Melt the chocolate in the water over gentle heat, add the sugar and salt and simmer, uncovered, until the sauce is syrupy and coats the back of a spoon. Take from heat, stir in the orange-soaked sugar cubes until dissolved; chill.

Pears Belle Hélène

4—5 even-sized Anjou or Bartlett pears
sugar syrup, made with 2 cups water, ½ cup sugar
1 vanilla bean, split
1½ cups orange chocolate sauce

Method
Have the sugar syrup ready in a deep pan. Pare the pears and, from the bottom, scoop out the cores with a teaspoon. Set the pears in the sugar syrup with the vanilla bean (add more water if they are not covered), cover pan and poach gently for 20—30 minutes or until the pears are tender. Cool them in the syrup. Be sure the pears are thoroughly cooked or they will discolor after they are drained.

To serve, drain the pears, set them on a platter or in an attractive dish and spoon over the orange chocolate sauce.

Chocolate and Caramel Rice

4 squares (4 oz) semisweet
   chocolate
3 cups milk
¼ cup rice
½ vanilla bean, split or
   ½ teaspoon vanilla extract
1–2 tablespoons sugar
   (or to taste)
1 egg
2 egg yolks
½ tablespoon butter
1 cup hot chocolate sauce,
   or 1½ cups crème à la vanille
   (for serving)

For caramel
½ cup sugar
½ cup water

*Charlotte mold, or soufflé dish
   (1 quart capacity)*

Method
To make the caramel: dissolve
the sugar in the water over
gentle heat, bring to a boil and
boil rapidly without stirring
until syrup is a rich brown.
Stop it cooking by dipping the
base of the pan into a bowl of
cold water; when no longer
bubbling, pour caramel into
the dry, warm mold or dish
and tilt it around gently to coat
the bottom and part way up
the sides.

Cut up or grate the chocolate, put it in a pan with the
milk and heat gently, stirring
occasionally, until melted.
Add the rice and vanilla bean,
if using, and simmer 30–35
minutes or until rice is tender
and all the milk is absorbed —
the mixture should drop easily
from a spoon. Stir the rice
occasionally and if the mixture
looks dry before the rice is
tender, add more milk. Set
oven at moderate (350°F).

Take pan from heat, remove
vanilla bean or add the vanilla
extract and stir in sugar to
taste. Beat in the egg, egg

yolks and butter and pour into
the caramel-lined mold or dish.
Cover securely with a piece of
buttered foil and set in a
water bath. Bake in heated
oven for 45–50 minutes or
until the tip of a knife inserted
in the center comes out clean.
Cool slightly, turn out onto a
platter and pour hot chocolate sauce or crème à la vanille
around it or serve separately.

Crème à la Vanille (Vanilla Custard Sauce)

1½ cups milk
2 tablespoons sugar
½ teaspoon vanilla extract or
   ½ vanilla bean, split
3 egg yolks

Method
Put milk in a pan with sugar
and heat until dissolved; if
using vanilla bean, infuse it
in the milk for 10 minutes,
keeping pan covered. Take
out bean, then add the sugar.

Beat egg yolks in a bowl
until lightly colored, scald
the vanilla-flavored milk and
gradually stir into yolks.
Return to pan and stir with a
wooden spoon over gentle
heat. When custard coats
back of spoon and looks
creamy, strain back into bowl.
Add the vanilla if using.
Sprinkle with a little sugar
and cool. This coating of
sugar melts and helps to
prevent a skin from forming.
Watchpoint: if the custard
gets too hot and starts to
curdle, pour it at once into
the bowl without straining
and whisk briskly for 10
seconds.

Suprême de Chocolat

6 squares (6 oz) semisweet
   chocolate
6 tablespoons unsalted butter
5–6 tablespoons sugar
4 eggs, separated
1 tablespoon brandy or
   2 tablespoons sherry
1½ cups crème à la vanille
   (for serving)

*Charlotte mold, or soufflé dish
   (1 quart capacity)*

Method
Lightly oil mold or dish. Cut up
and melt chocolate on a heatproof plate over a pan of hot
water and let it cool. Cream
butter, gradually beat in sugar
and beat until light and soft.
Beat in egg yolks, one at a
time. Beat egg whites until
they hold a stiff peak.

Stir the cool but still liquid
chocolate quickly into egg
yolk mixture with brandy or
sherry and fold in egg whites.
Transfer to the prepared mold
or dish, smooth the top and
chill 12 hours or overnight in
the refrigerator.

To serve, turn out suprême
de chocolat onto a platter.
Pour the chilled crème à la
vanille around it or serve it
separately.

Sugar Syrup
For 1 cup: in a pan heat
gently 1 cup sugar and
¾ cup water until sugar is
dissolved. Bring to a boil
and cook steadily for 3–4
minutes (220°F on a
sugar thermometer). Cool
and store in a screwtop
jar.

Chocolate and Strawberry Gâteau

12 squares (12 oz) semisweet
   chocolate
1 pint fresh strawberries
½ cup sugar syrup, flavored
   with vanilla, rum or sherry
1 cup heavy cream, whipped
   until it holds a soft shape

For sponge cake
½ cup flour
¼ teaspoon salt
2 eggs
½ cup sugar

*8–9 inch cake pan; 6–7 inch
   springform pan*

Method
Line bottom and sides of the
cake pan with foil. Grease the
springform pan, sprinkle it
with sugar, then with flour,
discarding the excess.

To make chocolate case:
cut up and melt chocolate on
a heatproof plate over a pan
of hot water. Take from heat,
cool a little and work with a
metal spatula until thick
enough to spread. Spread the
sides and bottom of the foil-
lined cake pan fairly thickly
with chocolate, using the back
of a spoon; coat sides well.
Chill 1–2 hours or until set.

Set oven at moderate
(350°F).

To make the sponge cake:
sift the flour and salt 3–4
times. Put the eggs in a bowl
and gradually beat in the
sugar. Set the bowl over a pan
of hot water and beat until the
mixture is light and leaves a
ribbon trail. If using an electric beater, no heat is necessary.

With a metal spoon, fold
the flour into the mixture, pour
the batter into the prepared
pan and bake in heated oven
for 20–25 minutes or until the

Chocolate and strawberry gâteau – a strawberry-filled sponge cake is set in a chocolate case

cake springs back when lightly pressed with a fingertip. Turn out onto a wire rack to cool.

To remove the foil from chocolate case: lift the case from the pan and start to peel and bend the foil out and away from the chocolate. Continue until most of the sides and bottom are free,

keeping your hand on the outside of the foil to keep from touching the chocolate. Slide the case onto a wire rack and remove the remaining foil.

Split the sponge cake in half, lay one half in the chocolate case and spoon over half the cold sugar syrup to soak it thoroughly.

Hull most of the strawberries, reserving the unhulled ones for decoration, and slice the rest. Moisten them with 1–2 tablespoons sugar syrup and put on top of the sponge cake. Cover with a layer of cream, top with the other half of cake and spoon over the remaining sugar syrup.

Pile remaining cream on top and decorate with the reserved strawberries.

Magali

½ cup quantity of French flan
   pastry or pastry trimmings
   (see Volume 3)
½ cup ganache cream
½ cup fondant icing (see
   page 102) or glacé icing,
   flavored with 1 square (1 oz)
   melted semisweet chocolate
2 tablespoons whole blanched
   almonds, browned and
   ground
1 tablespoon slivered almonds,
   browned

10–12 tartlet pans (1½–2 inch)

Method

Set oven at moderate (350°F).
   Roll out the pastry dough
thinly, line the tartlet pans,
prick the bottoms and chill
15 minutes. Bake blind in
heated oven for 12–15
minutes or until lightly
browned. Let cool.
   Fill the tartlets level to the
tops with ganache cream. Let
stand until the cream is fairly
firm, then remove from the
pans and coat with icing.
Decorate top edges with
ground almonds and place a
slivered almond in the center
of each.

Ganache Cream

For ½ cup, chop 2½
squares (2½ oz) semisweet
chocolate and melt in a
pan with 1 tablespoon
unsalted butter and ¼ cup
heavy cream. Cook until
thick, beating well. Add
2 teaspoons rum and let
cool. If the mixture sepa-
rates, stir in a few drops
of cold water.

Galettes Muscats
(Oak Leaf Cookies)

3 squares (3 oz) semisweet
   chocolate (for coating)
1 cup whole blanched almonds,
   ground
¾ cup sugar
½ teaspoon vanilla
2–3 egg whites

*Cardboard stencil of an
oak leaf*

Makes 12 cookies.

Method

Sift the ground almonds and
sugar together through a
coarse strainer. Beat the egg
whites and vanilla with a fork
until lightly mixed and stir
enough into the almonds and
sugar to make a firm but
spreadable paste.
   Set the oven at moderate
(350°F). Grease and flour 2
baking sheets.
   Place the stencil on a
baking sheet and spread the
mixture inside it; lift up the
stencil sharply to give a clean
edge. Repeat until all the
mixture is used.
   Bake the cookies in heated
oven for 10–12 minutes or
until lightly browned. Lift
them from baking sheets with
a sharp knife and transfer to
a wire rack to cool.
   Cut up and melt the chocolate on a heatproof plate over
a pan of hot water and, while
it is melting, work with a
metal spatula until smooth.
Cool slightly, then spread the
chocolate over the smooth
(under) side of the cold
cookies. Leave until the
chocolate is on the point of
setting, then mark veins on
the chocolate-coated side of
the 'leaves' with the point of
a knife. Chill until set.

To make a Cardboard Stencil

Take a piece of thin cardboard about 4½ X 3½
inches (a post card is
ideal) and in pencil draw
an oak leaf about 3½ X
2–2½ inches. Cut out the
leaf with scissors. Bend
up one corner of the card
so the stencil is easy to
lift.
   Stencils can also be cut
in the shape of flowers or
a circle, either for placing
on top of a sponge cake
before sprinkling with
confectioners' sugar or
for shaping cookies as in
galettes muscats.

Rich Chocolate Sauce

For 1 cup: cut up 2 squares
(2 oz) semisweet chocolate
and put in a saucepan with
2 tablespoons sugar, 1 teaspoon cocoa, 1 teaspoon dry
instant coffee and 1½ cups
water. Heat slowly, stirring
frequently until dissolved,
then simmer, uncovered, for
20 minutes or until it is the
consistency of heavy cream.
   Take from heat and stir 1–2
tablespoons sauce into 1 egg
yolk; return to pan and add
1 teaspoon vanilla. If not
using an egg yolk, simmer the
sauce until it is a little thicker
before adding the vanilla.
Serve hot or cold.

Charlotte Mexicaine

6 squares (6 oz) semisweet
   chocolate
2½ cups milk
½ cup coarsely ground coffee
5 egg yolks
¼ cup sugar
1 envelope gelatin
¼ cup water
1 egg white
1 cup heavy cream, whipped
   until it holds a soft shape

For decoration
1 cup heavy cream, stiffly
   whipped
12–15 cats' tongues cookies or
   ladyfingers
squares or rounds of chocolate
   (optional)

*Charlotte mold, or soufflé dish
(1½ quart capacity); pastry
bag and a medium star tube*

Method

Lightly oil the mold or dish.
   Scald the milk with the
ground coffee, cover and let
stand to infuse for 10–15
minutes until well flavored.
   Cut up and put the chocolate in a pan and strain in
about 1 cup of the coffee-
flavored milk. Melt the chocolate over gentle heat, strain in
remaining milk and mix well.
Beat the egg yolks and sugar
until thick and light, stir in
the milk and return the mixture to the pan. Heat, stirring,
until the custard thickens
enough to coat the back of a
wooden spoon; do not let it
boil. Strain.
   Sprinkle the gelatin over the
water in a cup or bowl, let
stand 5 minutes until spongy
and stir into the hot custard
until dissolved. Cool the mixture, then set over ice and stir
until it is on the point of
setting.
   Beat the egg white until it
holds a stiff peak. Fold the

lightly whipped cream into the chocolate mixture, followed by the egg white and pour into the prepared mold or dish. Chill at least 2 hours or until set.

To serve, turn out the charlotte onto a platter, spread the sides with a little whipped cream and arrange the cookies or ladyfingers, overlapping, around the sides. Decorate the top with rosettes of the remaining cream, using a pastry bag fitted with a star tube, and, if you like, with squares or rounds of chocolate.

A cake decorating comb is a flat piece of metal or plastic with indentations like a comb at one side. When drawn over chocolate on the point of setting, it gives a decorative pattern. Or you can use a clean, regular comb with wide teeth.

Florentines

3 tablespoons butter
½ cup heavy cream
½ cup sugar
¼ cup candied cherries, cut in quarters
1 cup blanched almonds, finely chopped
6 tablespoons shredded almonds
¾ cup candied orange peel, finely chopped
⅓ cup flour
4 squares (4 oz) semisweet chocolate

3 inch plain cookie cutter; cake decorating comb (optional)

Makes about 20 cookies.

Method
Grease a baking sheet and set oven at moderate (350°F).

Melt the butter with the cream and sugar and bring slowly to a boil. Take from heat and stir in the cherries, chopped and shredded almonds, candied peel and flour. Drop spoonsful of mixture onto the prepared baking sheet, leaving space between each for cookies to spread, and flatten each with a wet fork.

Bake in heated oven for 5–6 minutes. Take from oven and, with cookie cutter, pull the edges of each cookie together inside the cutter. Return to oven and bake 5–6 minutes longer or until lightly browned at the edges. Cool a little on the baking sheet, then remove the cookies with a sharp knife and let cool completely on a wire rack.

Cut up and melt the chocolate on a heatproof plate over a pan of hot water. Cool a little, then work with a metal spatula until smooth and thick. Spread the smooth (under) sides of the cookies with chocolate and, if you like,

when on the point of setting, work it in wavy lines with a cake decorating comb.

After preliminary baking, pull ▶ the edges of Florentine cookies together inside cookie cutter

Work chocolate in wavy lines with a cake decorating comb ▶

Rich Gâteau au Chocolat

8 squares (8 oz) semisweet
    chocolate
¾ cup flour
pinch of salt
1 teaspoon baking powder
1 cup butter
1 cup sugar
7 eggs, separated
⅔ cup whole blanched almonds,
    ground

For coating
2 cups fondant icing, flavored
    with 1 teaspoon rum
½ cup apricot jam glaze
    (see Volume 2)

8 inch springform pan

Method
Line the pan with a circle of
wax paper and grease base
and sides of pan. Set oven at
moderate (350°F).

Sift the flour with the salt
and baking powder. Cut up
and melt the chocolate on a
heatproof plate over a pan of
hot water; cool. Cream the
butter, gradually add the
sugar and beat until the mixture is light and fluffy. Beat in
the egg yolks, one at a time,
then stir in the cool but still
liquid chocolate and ground
almonds. Beat the egg whites
until they hold a stiff peak and
fold them into the mixture
alternately with the sifted
flour.

Transfer the mixture to the
prepared pan and bake in
heated oven for 30 minutes.
Reduce heat to moderately
hot (325°F) and bake 30–40
minutes longer or until a
toothpick inserted in the
center comes out clean. Cool
slightly, then turn out onto a
wire rack to cool completely.
Brush the cake with warm
apricot jam glaze and, when
set, coat with melted fondant
icing.

Fondant Icing

2 cups sugar
¾ cup water
2 tablespoons corn syrup, or
    pinch of cream of tartar
    (dissolved in 1 teaspoon
    water)

Sugar thermometer

Makes about 2 cups (enough
icing to cover an 8–9 inch
cake).

Method
Place the sugar and water in
a saucepan and heat gently
until the sugar is dissolved.
Add the corn syrup or dissolved cream of tartar, bring
to a boil and boil steadily to
the soft ball stage (240°F on
a sugar thermometer). Take
the pan at once from the heat,
let the bubbles subside and
pour the mixture slowly onto a
dampened marble slab or into
a dampened roasting pan.

Cook the mixture slightly,
add the chosen flavoring and
then pull the batch together
with a sugar scraper or metal
spatula, taking the mixture
from the edge to the center.
Leave until the fondant feels
just warm to the touch. If
using a roasting pan, turn out
onto a Formica-type surface.
Work vigorously with a sugar
scraper or metal spatula in
one hand and a wooden
spoon in the other, turning
and pulling it to the
center until it becomes creamy
– it will do this very suddenly
and will become too stiff to
work.

Then take a small piece of
fondant at a time and work it
with the fingers until smooth.
Pack into a bowl, cover tightly
and leave 1 hour and preferably 2–3 days to mellow.

To use the icing: put
fondant in the top of a double
boiler or in a bowl over a pan
of hot water. Add 1–2 tablespoons sugar syrup and heat
fondant until it is just lukewarm, stirring it constantly;
add more sugar syrup as
necessary so the warm
fondant coats the back of a
spoon.

Watchpoint: do not let the
fondant heat above lukewarm
or it will lose its gloss.

Use fondant icing while still
melted; do not continue
working it on top of a cake
after it starts to set or the
finish will be rough.

To make Chocolate Squares and Rounds
Cut or chop 3 squares (3 oz)
semisweet chocolate into
pieces and melt on a heatproof plate over a pan of hot
water, working with a metal
spatula until it is smooth
but not hot.

For squares: spread the
chocolate evenly and thinly
(about one-eighth inch thick)
over an 8 inch wax paper
square and, when on the point
of setting, mark into squares
with a sharp knife.

For rounds: cut wax paper
circles the required size and
spread them with chocolate.

Refrigerate until hard (about
1 hour), then peel away wax
paper.

Chocolate Roulade

6 squares (6 oz) semisweet
    chocolate
3–4 tablespoons water
5 eggs, separated
1 cup sugar
confectioners' sugar
    (for sprinkling)

For filling
1½ cups heavy cream, whipped
    until it holds a soft shape and
    flavored with vanilla, rum or
    brandy

*15 X 10 inch jelly roll pan
    or paper case*

If you like, the cream filling
can be mixed with 1 cup of
cooked, sieved, dry chestnuts.

Method
Line the pan with wax paper
and grease it or the paper
case. Set oven at moderate
(350°F).

Cut up and melt the chocolate in the water in a pan over
very gentle heat, stirring until
thick and creamy. Cool. Beat
the egg yolks with sugar for
about 5 minutes or until the
mixture is thick and light.
Beat the egg whites until they
hold a stiff peak. Stir the
cooled chocolate into egg
yolk mixture, then fold in egg
whites as lightly as possible.

Spread the mixture in the
prepared pan or paper case
and bake in heated oven for
15 minutes or until the mixture springs back when lightly
pressed with a fingertip.

Have a clean dish towel
ready, wrung out in cold
water. Take out the roulade,
cool it slightly, then cover with
the cloth (this prevents any
sugary crust from forming). To
give the cake a velvety texture
leave for 12 hours or overnight in refrigerator.

Sprinkle a sheet of wax

For rich party desserts make a chocolate roulade, left, or nègre en chemise with chocolate rounds and a cream ruff

paper with confectioners' sugar. Remove the cloth and turn the roulade upside down on the prepared paper. Remove the pan or paper case, trim the edges of the roulade, spread with whipped cream and roll up like a jelly roll. Transfer to a platter and sprinkle generously with confectioners' sugar.

Stir the melted chocolate into the egg mixture for roulade

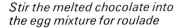

Decorate nègre en chemise with a few chocolate rounds

Nègre en Chemise

12 squares (12 oz) semisweet chocolate
½ cup water
6 tablespoons unsalted butter
½ cup praline powder
1–2 tablespoons brandy or rum
1 cup heavy cream, whipped until it holds a soft shape

For decoration
1–1½ cups heavy cream, stiffly whipped
rounds of chocolate

Bombe mold or round metal bowl (1 quart capacity); pastry bag and a medium star tube

Method
Cup up and melt the chocolate in the water over gentle heat, stirring until the mixture is thick and creamy. Take from

heat and cool.

Cream the butter, beat in the cool but still liquid chocolate and gradually beat in the praline powder. Flavor to taste with brandy or rum.

Lightly oil the mold or bowl. Fold the lightly whipped cream into the chocolate mixture and fill the mold or bowl. Chill 2–3 hours or until set.

To serve: loosen the chocolate mold by dipping it quickly in hot water and turn out onto a platter. Put the stiffly whipped cream into the pastry bag fitted with the star tube and pipe a ruff of cream around the edge of the mold. Decorate with rounds of chocolate.

Praline Powder

To make about ½ cup praline powder: put ½ cup unblanched almonds with ½ cup sugar in a heavy-based pan. Cook over low heat until the sugar melts, shaking the pan occasionally. When the sugar turns a pale golden brown, stir the mixture with a metal spoon and continue cooking until it is dark brown but do not let it burn. Pour at once onto an oiled baking sheet and leave until cold and hard. Grind in a rotary cheese grater or a grinder or work in a blender a little at a time.

Praline powder can be stored in an airtight container – it may become soft and sticky but the flavor will not be impaired.

A slice of fresh mincemeat pie (recipe is on page 109)

A FRESH APPROACH TO MINCEMEAT PIE

Start a simple menu with flounder and cucumber or make a broth from turkey or chicken leftovers. Then braise a stuffed leg of lamb, and finish with fresh mincemeat pie.

With the authoritative flavors of anchovy and ham used in the stuffing for the leg of lamb, a correspondingly forthright wine is in order. Those wines from the northernmost district of the Rhône Valley, the Côte Rôtie, certainly have this character; they exhibit a splendid bouquet, some say reminiscent of violets. An equally full-flavored, if not so distinguished, wine is the Petit Syrah, most frequently raised in the vineyards north of San Francisco.

Flounder with Cucumber
or
Chicken or Turkey Broth

Braised Stuffed Leg of Lamb
Broccoli Mold
Château Potatoes

Fresh Mincemeat Pie

∾

Red wine — Côte Rôtie (Rhône)
or Petit Syrah (California)

TIMETABLE

Day before
Make the mincemeat, refrigerate in covered container. Make pie pastry dough and keep in plastic wrap in refrigerator.
Make the stock for lamb *and for broth.* Cover and refrigerate.

Morning
Prepare fish and put in dish for cooking; cut and blanch cucumber and put in pan with butter.
Make broth but do not add cream or parsley.
Prepare broccoli mold, leave in mold until ready to cook.
Stuff and lard meat, cover and refrigerate.
Dice the vegetables for the lamb and make the sauce.
Line pie pan and bake the mincemeat pie. Cool, then keep covered.

Assemble equipment for final cooking from 5:30 for dinner around 8 p.m.

Order of Work
5:30
Set oven at moderate (350°F); heat oil in casserole, brown meat, take out, add the vegetables and brown. Replace meat, add the rest of the ingredients, flame the wine and bring to a boil.
5:45
Cover the casserole and put in oven.
6:50
Brown the potatoes (blanch first, if necessary) and put in top of oven. Whip and flavor cream for pie, cover and refrigerate.

7:15
Put fish into oven on the shelf under the meat. Remove potatoes and keep warm. Put broccoli mold into oven beside meat.
7:30
Remove fish and strain liquid. Cook cucumber in butter on top of stove. Make sauce for fish and keep both warm.
7:45
Remove meat, strain off the liquid and put meat back in oven to keep warm. Reduce liquid and add to prepared sauce; heat and keep hot.
Remove the broccoli mold and turn oven very low (200°F). Turn out broccoli mold onto platter but do not lift off the mold; keep hot.
Coat the fish with sauce, sprinkle with cheese and brown under broiler, *or heat broth.*
8:00
Garnish the fish with the cucumber and herb mixture, *or add cream and parsley to broth* and serve. When entrée is served, put mincemeat pie back in oven to heat. Add whipped cream just before serving.

You will find that **cooking times** given in the individual recipes for these dishes have sometimes been adapted in the timetable to help you when cooking and serving this menu as a party meal.

Appetizer

Flounder with Cucumber

4–6 (1½ lb) flounder fillets
grated rind and juice of ½ lemon
¾ cup water
salt and pepper
5–6 peppercorns

For garnish
2 cucumbers, peeled and cut in chunks
1 tablespoon butter
1 tablespoon chopped fresh dill, mint or parsley
1 tablespoon grated Gruyère cheese

For sauce
2 tablespoons butter
1½ tablespoons flour
¾ cup milk

Method
Wash the flounder fillets and dry on paper towels. Tuck under the ends of the fillets, place in a buttered ovenproof dish, pour on the lemon juice and water and sprinkle over the lemon rind. Season with salt and add the peppercorns, cover with foil and poach in a moderately low oven (325°F) for 15 minutes or until tender.

Drain the fillets, then arrange on a heatproof platter and keep hot. Reserve the cooking liquid.

To prepare the garnish: blanch the cucumber chunks in boiling salted water for 1 minute, then drain. In a saucepan, melt the butter, add the cucumber and season to taste. Cover and cook the cucumber chunks over low heat for 5 minutes or until barely tender. Keep warm.

To make the sauce: melt the butter in a saucepan, blend in the flour off the heat and stir in the strained liquid from the fish. Bring to a boil, stirring until thickened, then add the milk. Boil the sauce until it is reduced to the consistency of heavy cream and taste for seasoning.

Spoon the sauce over the fish, sprinkle with grated cheese and brown lightly under the broiler. Garnish with the cucumber mixed with the chopped herbs.

When you have a turkey or ▶ chicken, be sure to use the carcass bones for making stock. This makes a delicious soup if you add cream and sprinkle a little chopped parsley over each bowl

Alternative appetizer

Chicken or Turkey Broth

raw or cooked turkey or
  chicken carcass bones
3 tablespoons finely diced
  carrot (discard the yellow
  core)
2 tablespoons finely chopped
  onion
salt and pepper
2 tablespoons rice
3–4 tablespoons heavy cream
1 tablespoon chopped parsley

Method
To make the stock from turkey
or chicken carcass bones: add
just enough water to cover
them and simmer gently for
2–3 hours. For a strong, clear
stock, do not boil. Strain and
chill; remove all fat.

Put 1 quart of the stock
with the carrot and onion in
a saucepan, season, cover
and simmer for 10 minutes.
Add rice and cook 12 min-
utes longer or until the vegetables and rice are tender.
Taste for seasoning.

Spoon the broth into individual bowls, add cream and
sprinkle with parsley; serve.

Entrée

Braised Stuffed Leg of Lamb

1 small (4–5 lb) leg of lamb
8 anchovy fillets
3 tablespoons milk (for soaking
  anchovies)
½ lb cooked ham, sliced
1 shallot, finely chopped
1 tablespoon chopped parsley
pinch of thyme or marjoram

For braising
1–2 tablespoons oil
2 carrots, diced
2 onions, diced
2–3 stalks of celery, diced
2 cloves of garlic
½ cup red wine (optional)
1½ cups brown stock
bouquet garni

For sauce
2 tablespoons butter
2 shallots, finely chopped
1 tablespoon flour
2 teaspoons tomato paste
2 cups brown stock
salt and pepper

*Trussing needle and string;
  larding needle*

Method
Have your butcher bone the
leg of lamb without cutting
the skin. Soak half the anchovies in the milk to remove
excess salt. Lay the ham
slices overlapping on a board,
drain the anchovy fillets and
place them on top. Sprinkle
with the shallot and herbs and
roll up to form a cylinder.
Push this into the boned
lamb and sew up with the
trussing needle and string.
Lard the meat with the remaining anchovies by sewing
them into the meat with the
larding needle (see Volume 2).

Heat the oil in a heavy
flameproof casserole, brown
the meat lightly on all sides
and remove it. Add the vegetables, cover the pot, reduce
the heat and cook gently for
8–10 minutes or until the
vegetables are lightly browned
and have absorbed all the fat.

Place the leg of lamb on
the vegetables, add the garlic
and wine, heat and flame it.
Add the stock and bouquet
garni and bring to a boil.
Cover the pot and braise in a
moderate oven (350°F) for
2 hours or until the lamb is
very tender.

To make the sauce: melt
the butter in a saucepan, add
the shallot, cook slowly until
soft, then stir in the flour and
brown it over medium heat.
Stir in the tomato paste and
stock, bring to a boil and
simmer, stirring occasionally,
for 30–40 minutes or until
it is reduced to about 1 cup.

Take the meat from the
oven, strain the cooking
liquid and boil to reduce it to
½ cup. Add this to the sauce
and taste for seasoning.

Remove the strings from
the meat, arrange it on a platter and spoon over a little of
the sauce. Pour the rest of the
sauce into a sauce boat and
serve separately.

*To stuff the boned leg of
lamb, place the anchovy fillets
on the ham slices, sprinkle
with shallot and herbs and roll
up into a cylinder*

*Push the ham cylinder into the
boned lamb and sew up with a
trussing needle and string;
then lard the meat with the
remaining anchovies*

Left: coat flounder fillets in sauce, sprinkle with cheese and brown under the broiler before garnishing with the cucumber and herb mixture

Below left: serve braised stuffed leg of lamb with a broccoli mold and château potatoes, and mincemeat pie with whipped cream for dessert

Accompaniments to entrée

Château Potatoes

10–12 small new potatoes,
   or 3–4 medium potatoes
3–4 tablespoons butter
salt

Method
If using medium potatoes, peel them, cut in quarters lengthwise and trim off the sharp edges with a vegetable peeler. Blanch them by putting in cold water and bringing to a boil, then drain. If using new potatoes, scrub them with a pot scrubber or small brush to remove the skin, or use a vegetable peeler.

In a flameproof casserole melt the butter, add the potatoes and cook over moderate heat until golden brown all over, occasionally shaking to turn them and prevent them from sticking. Sprinkle lightly with salt, cover and bake in a hot oven (400°F) for 10–12 minutes or until tender.

Broccoli Mold

1 bunch of fresh broccoli or
   2 packages frozen broccoli
½ cup hot milk
1 cup fresh white breadcrumbs
3 tablespoons butter
1 egg yolk
grated nutmeg (to taste)
salt and pepper

*Cake pan, or ring mold
(1 quart capacity)*

Method
Butter the cake pan or ring mold.

Peel thick stems of fresh broccoli with a vegetable peeler to remove the hard outside skin, trim the ends and cut large stems in half.

Cook the broccoli in plenty of boiling salted water for 8–10 minutes or until tender. Drain, refresh and drain again; shake to remove excess water. Cook frozen broccoli according to the package directions. Purée the cooked broccoli in a blender or work it through a sieve or food mill. Soak the breadcrumbs in hot milk.

Put the broccoli in a pan, add the butter, a small piece at a time, and stir over heat until the purée pulls away from the sides of the pan. Take from heat, add the soaked crumbs, egg yolk and nutmeg and season well. Pour the purée into the prepared pan or mold, cover with foil and stand in a water bath. Bake in a moderate oven (350°F) for 40 minutes or until firm. Let stand a few minutes before unmolding onto a plate. Serve plain, or coated with a white or cheese sauce (see Volume 2).

Dessert

Fresh Mincemeat Pie

For rich pie pastry
2 cups flour
½ teaspoon salt
⅔ cup butter
2 teaspoons sugar
1 egg yolk
3–4 tablespoons cold water

For fresh mincemeat
2 medium dessert apples,
   pared, cored and chopped
3 tablespoons chopped candied
   orange peel
1½ cups raisins
1 cup currants
⅔ cup golden raisins
1 cup (½ lb) seedless green
   grapes
¼ cup shredded almonds
grated rind and juice of
   1 small lemon
¼ teaspoon ground allspice
1½ cups dark brown sugar
2 tablespoons melted butter
¼ cup brandy or sherry

To finish
sugar (for sprinkling)
½ cup heavy cream, whipped
   until it holds a stiff peak
1 tablespoon rum or brandy

*9 inch flan ring, or pie pan
with removable base; 3 inch
plain cookie cutter*

This quantity of mincemeat makes two 9 inch pies; the pastry is enough for 1 pie. If making 1 pie, the leftover mincemeat can be stored in a covered container in the refrigerator for up to 2 weeks.

Method
Prepare the pastry dough (see Volume 1) and chill 30 minutes.

To make the mincemeat: combine all the ingredients in a bowl; if the grapes are large, cut them into 2–3 pieces.

Set the oven at moderately hot (375°F).

Roll out two-thirds of the pastry dough, line the flan ring or pie pan and fill it with mincemeat. Roll out the remaining dough to a 9 inch circle and stamp out a hole in the middle with the plain cutter. Put the dough ring on top of the filled pie and flute the edges to decorate and seal them. Brush with water and sprinkle with sugar.

Bake the pie in heated oven for 30–40 minutes or until the pastry is brown and the mincemeat is bubbling hot.

Flavor the stiffly whipped cream with rum or brandy, pile into the middle of the pie and serve at once.

Lay the pastry dough ring on top of the pie, filled with fresh mincemeat, and flute the edges to seal

Two traditional foods eaten at Easter are kulich (left), a rich yeast bread, and paskha, a cheese and sugar mixture molded in a pyramid (recipes are on page 119)

RUSSIAN COOKING

Russian cooking is as diverse as the country itself. Climates range from the bitter Siberian steppes where snow covers the ground for nine months of the year to the benign Mediterranean breezes of the Black Sea resorts. Local ingredients and dishes vary accordingly.

The Slavic regions of northern Russia — from the Urals to Leningrad — are famous for their baking. Honey and poppyseeds are plentiful and Kulich or Easter Baba bread are said to have originated there.

The Lithuanian and Baltic areas of the west are known for the richness of their ingredients — sour cream, butter, eggs, ham and sausages. As in most of Russia, root vegetables like carrots, potatoes and beets are staples because the summer season for green vegetables is short. Cabbage is a favorite, both fresh and made into sauerkraut, and the Russian love of pickles blossoms into a wealth of pickled cucumbers, beets and herring. The influence of nearby Scandinavia is shown in fruit soups, the use of herring and the popularity of cold buffets similar to smørrebrød.

Both near the Baltic and in northern Russia, wheat is the dominant grain. South in the Caucasus, the climate is much warmer and the food is more like that of Greece and Turkey — rich pastries, plenty of fresh salads and vegetables, and yogurt and rice rather than milk and wheat. Spices are popular but not nearly so vital as farther east in Turkestan, where the cooking is typically Asian with pilaf as the universal dish and lamb the staple meat. In the east the food still shows the influence of the nomadic habits of the ancient tribes — many dishes are steamed and few need exact timing or elaborate preparation.

Overlying the peasant simplicity of regional Russian cooking are the memories of sophisticated dishes served to the Tsars. For example, kulebiaka, pojarski and charlotte russe were created by French chefs at the glittering Court of the Tsars and are still well-known in Russia today.

Despite the regional diversity, some dishes are as unmistakably Russian as vodka — piroshki (little pastries with savory fillings), bortsch, blini (a kind of pancake) and kasha, and all are characteristic of a hearty but refined style typical of Russian cooking.

Zakouski

This Russian equivalent of our hot and cold hors d'œuvre can vary from a selection of elegant little canapés to a huge spread reminiscent of smørrebrød. Serve a selection from the following: pickled mushrooms, radishes in sour cream, pickled cucumbers, chicken liver pâté, salted and pickled herring or stuffed peppers.

Sour Cream Horseradish Sauce

Mix 1 cup sour cream with 1–2 tablespoons grated fresh horseradish. Serve with the beef used to make bortsch (see recipe).

Solianka
(Fish Soup)

1 lb firm white fish fillets such as cod or haddock, cut in chunks
1 cucumber
salt
2 medium onions, chopped
1 tablespoon chopped capers
¼ cup green olives, pitted and chopped

For fish stock
1 lb fish bones
6 cups water
1 onion, sliced
bouquet garni
6 peppercorns

For garnish
1 lemon, cut in thin slices
⅓ cup ripe olives, pitted and chopped
¼ cup chopped parsley

Method
Peel and halve the cucumber, and scoop out the seeds. Slice it thinly, sprinkle with salt, cover and let stand in refrigerator for 12 hours. Drain the slices, rinse with cold water and drain well.

To make the fish stock: in a kettle combine the fish bones, water, onion, bouquet garni and peppercorns. Cover, simmer 20 minutes and strain.

Add the onion, capers, cucumber and green olives to the strained liquid; cover and simmer 20 minutes. Add the fish chunks and simmer 5 minutes or just until the fish flakes easily when tested with a fork.

Serve the soup at once and garnish each bowl with 2–3 slices of lemon and a sprinkling of olives and parsley.

Russian bortsch with sour cream is served with piroshki — pastries made with sour cream

Bortsch is a beet soup that originated in the Ukraine; the name is an old Slav word for beet. There are innumerable Russian versions — some are a clear, deep red broth called **borshchok**; others are more like a stew with added meat and vegetables, particularly cabbage. They should be flavored with lemon juice and served with sour cream.

Russian Bortsch

2–2½ lb round or rump roast of
  beef
3 quarts water
6 peppercorns
1 bay leaf
3 medium beets, scrubbed and
  trimmed
juice of ½ lemon
salt
about 1 tablespoon sugar (to
  taste)

For garnish
½ cup sour cream
1 tablespoon chopped fresh
  dill (optional)

The beef used to make
bortsch is removed as soon as
it is cooked, leaving only the
pot juices. The beef can then
be served as a course on its
own with boiled root vegetables and sour cream horseradish sauce, or it can be cut
in small cubes and returned
to the finished soup.
  Piroshki (beef- or vegetable-
filled pastries) are the traditional accompaniment to
bortsch.

Method
In a large casserole put the
beef with the water, peppercorns and bay leaf, cover and
bring to a boil. Skim well,
cover and simmer 2–2½
hours or until the beef is
tender, skimming occasionally.
  Cook the beets in boiling,
salted water for 30–40 minutes, drain them and slip off
the skins with your fingers.
Cut the beets into small
chunks.
  When the beef is cooked,
remove it from the pot
together with the bay leaf and
reserve for future use. Add the
beets to the soup and simmer
5 minutes. Stir in the lemon
juice with salt and sugar to
taste — the bortsch should

have a sweet and sour, not
acid, flavor.
  Serve the soup in bowls
with a spoonful of sour cream
dropped in the center of each,
or serve separately. If you
like, sprinkle a little chopped
dill over the soup to garnish.

Piroshki

3½ cup quantity sour cream
  pastry
choice of filling (see right)
1 egg, beaten to mix with
  1 teaspoon salt

3–3½ inch plain cookie cutter

Serve as an accompaniment
to soups. Makes 36 piroshki
– enough for 8–10 people.

Method
Make the sour cream pastry
dough and chill 30 minutes.
Set oven at hot (400°F).
  Roll out dough on a floured
board about one-eighth inch
thick and stamp out 3–3½
inch rounds with a cookie
cutter.
  Place a spoonful of filling
in the center of each round,
brush the edges with beaten
egg and pinch them together
along the top of piroshki,
fluting (or scalloping) them
neatly.
  Transfer the piroshki to a
baking sheet, brush with
beaten egg and bake in heated
oven for 15–18 minutes or
until piroshki are golden
brown.

Fillings
for Piroshki

Fish

2 cups cooked fish, such as
  salmon or any white fish,
  flaked
1 onion, chopped
3 tablespoons butter
3 hard-cooked eggs
1 tablespoon chopped parsley
¼ teaspoon mace
salt and pepper

Makes enough to fill 36
piroshki.

Method
Cook the onion in the butter
until soft. Stir in the fish, hard-
cooked eggs, parsley, mace
and seasoning to taste.

Sour Cream Pastry

3 tablespoons sour cream
3½ cups flour
½ teaspoon salt
¾ cup butter
2 eggs, beaten to mix

Makes 3½ cup quantity.

Method
Sift the flour with the salt
into a bowl, add the butter
and rub in with the fingertips until the mixture
resembles fine bread-
crumbs. Add the beaten
eggs and sour cream. Stir,
then knead lightly to make
a fairly firm dough and
work it 1 minute with the
heel of the hand on a
floured board until it is
smooth and pliable. Chill
30 minutes before use.

Beef

1½ lb lean ground beef
1 onion, finely chopped
2 tablespoons butter
salt and pepper

Makes enough to fill 36
piroshki.

Method
In a skillet fry the onion in the
butter until soft. Add the
ground beef and cook over
medium heat, stirring to divide
up the meat, until it is
thoroughly browned. Season
well.

Cabbage

1 small cabbage, shredded
1 medium onion, finely chopped
2 tablespoons butter
3 hard-cooked eggs, finely
  chopped
salt and pepper

Makes enough to fill 36
piroshki.

Method
Put the cabbage in a colander
and pour a kettle of boiling
water over it. Refresh it with
cold water and drain
thoroughly. Fry the onion in
the butter and mix in the
cabbage, egg and plenty of
seasoning.

Serve blini hot, with caviar, and with a glass of vodka

Blini

1 cup flour
1½ cups buckwheat flour
2–2¼ cups milk
1 package dry or 1 cake
    compressed yeast
½ cup lukewarm water
½ teaspoon salt
3 eggs, separated
3 tablespoons melted butter
3 tablespoons sour cream

Blini take 5–6 hours to rise –
even longer than most
breads. Makes 36 blini.

Method
Scald the milk and cool it to
lukewarm. Sprinkle the yeast
over the lukewarm water and
let stand 5 minutes or until
dissolved.

Sift the flour with ¾ cup
buckwheat flour and the salt
into a bowl, make a well in
the center and add the yeast
mixture with 1 cup of the lukewarm milk. Stir, gradually
drawing in the flour to make a
smooth batter, beat well for 2
minutes, cover with a damp
cloth and let rise in a warm
place for 2–3 hours or until
the batter is light and full of
bubbles.

Beat the mixture to knock
out the air and beat in the
remaining buckwheat flour.
Cover and let rise again for
about 2 hours or until the
batter is doubled in bulk.

Beat in 1 cup more milk

until the batter is smooth,
then beat in the egg yolks,
melted butter and sour cream
and add a little more milk, if
necessary. The batter should
be the consistency of heavy
cream. Beat the egg whites
until they hold a stiff peak, fold
them into the batter and let
stand 30 minutes.

Heat a lightly buttered
griddle or heavy skillet and
pour in the batter with a
small ladle to make 3 inch
rounds. Cook 2–3 minutes
until the undersides of the blini
are lightly browned and the
tops are bubbling, then turn
and brown on other side.
Keep the blini warm while
cooking the rest of the batter
and serve the blini hot – they
do not reheat well. Suggestions for accompaniments are
given in the box, below.

Blini are most often asso-
ciated with caviar though
they can be served with
smoked salmon, smoked
sturgeon or salted herring.

Russians like to brush
the warm blini with salted
butter, then spread them
with caviar. Sour cream
may be served as well but
chopped hard-cooked egg
and chopped onion should
not be served as alter-
natives as they are
regarded as adulterants of
the pure flavor of caviar.

Blini are always eaten
the week before Lent.

Caucasian
Shoulder of
Lamb

3½–4 lb boned shoulder of
    lamb, tied in a cushion shape
2 cloves of garlic, cut in slivers
1 quart buttermilk
¼ cup yogurt
1 teaspoon ground coriander
½ teaspoon ground cumin
1 teaspoon oregano
½ teaspoon thyme
¼ teaspoon salt
¼ teaspoon black pepper,
    freshly ground
½ cup oil

Method
Pierce the lamb with the point
of a sharp knife and stud it
with slivers of garlic. Marinate
it in buttermilk in a heavy-
duty plastic bag or in a deep
bowl, covered, for 24–36
hours in the refrigerator. Discard the buttermilk and pat
the lamb dry with paper
towels.

Mix the yogurt with the
coriander, cumin, oregano,
thyme, salt and pepper and
spread the mixture over the
lamb.

Set the lamb in a roasting
pan, spoon over the oil and
roast in a moderately hot
oven (375°F) basting often for
1½–1¾ hours or until a meat
thermometer registers 160°F
for medium done meat.

Discard the strings and
serve the lamb with pilaf with
raisins and pistachios.

◀*When the blini are covered
with bubbles, turn them with a
spatula and brown other side*

Pojarski cotleti, ground veal shaped into cutlets, are fried and then covered with mushroom sauce

Pilaf with Raisins and Pistachios

1 cup rice
3 tablespoons oil
2–2$\frac{1}{2}$ cups stock
salt and pepper
$\frac{1}{2}$ cup raisins
$\frac{1}{2}$ cup shelled pistachios
3–4 scallions, sliced

Like shashlik, pilaf is designed to be cooked over an open fire; cooking is begun over very high heat, then the pilaf bakes more slowly as the fire dies down.

Method
In a flameproof casserole heat the oil and fry the rice gently until the grains are transparent. Pour on 2 cups stock, bring to a boil, cover and bake in a moderate oven (350°F) for 15 minutes.

Stir in the seasoning, raisins, pistachios and scallions and add a little more stock if the rice seems dry. Cover and continue baking the pilaf for 5–7 minutes or until all liquid is absorbed and the rice is tender. Let stand 10 minutes before removing the cover and stirring the rice.

Pojarski was an innkeeper at Torzhok, a town between Moscow and Leningrad. He invented these cutlets for his guests. Originally they were made with partridge or other available game or poultry.

Pojarski Cotleti

1$\frac{1}{2}$ lb veal round
salt and pepper
1$\frac{1}{2}$ cups heavy cream
$\frac{1}{4}$ cup seasoned flour (made with $\frac{1}{4}$ teaspoon salt and a pinch of pepper)
3 tablespoons butter
$\frac{1}{2}$ cup white wine
2 cups ($\frac{1}{2}$ lb) mushrooms, sliced
juice of $\frac{1}{2}$ lemon
1 teaspoon arrowroot (mixed to a paste with 1 tablespoon water)
$\frac{1}{4}$ cup brandy

Pojarski cotleti (cutlets) can also be made with ground chicken.

Method
Pass the veal twice through the fine blade of the grinder, then beat it in a bowl with a wooden spoon or with the dough hook of an electric mixer for 5 minutes or until the veal draws from the sides of the bowl in a ball. Season well and gradually beat in $\frac{3}{4}$ cup of the cream.

Divide mixture into 7–8 equal portions; shape into even-sized 'cutlets' on a board sprinkled with seasoned flour.

In a skillet heat 2 tablespoons of the butter and fry the pojarski over medium heat for about 3 minutes on each side or until lightly browned and the cream starts bubbling to the top of the meat. Take out, arrange on a platter and keep warm. Deglaze the pan by adding the white wine and simmering until the pan juices are dissolved.

In a saucepan melt the remaining butter, add the mushrooms with lemon juice and salt and pepper, cover and cook over high heat for 1–2 minutes until the mushrooms are tender. Add the mushrooms with any liquid to the skillet, stir in the remaining cream and bring to a boil. Stir in the arrowroot paste and cook until the sauce thickens slightly. Stir in the brandy, taste for seasoning, spoon over the pojarski and serve with pilaf or kasha (see page 116).

Kasha

1 cup coarse cracked
   buckwheat
1 small egg, beaten to mix
2 cups stock or water
1 teaspoon ground cumin
1 teaspoon ground coriander
salt and pepper

When made with medium or coarse cracked wheat instead of buckwheat this is called bulgur (see Volume 4). Serve as an accompaniment instead of rice or potatoes, or as stuffing.

Method
In a flameproof casserole combine the buckwheat with the egg and cook over medium heat, stirring constantly, until each grain is dry and separate – this will take 10–15 minutes. Add the stock or water with the spices and salt and pepper to taste, cover and bake in a moderate oven (350°F) for 20–30 minutes or until all the liquid is absorbed and the buckwheat is tender. Leave 15–20 minutes in a warm place or in a very low oven before serving so the starch grains contract and the kasha is not mushy.

Shashlik

2 lb boned lean leg or shoulder
   of lamb, cut in 1½ inch
   cubes

For marinade
1 medium onion, grated
juice of 1 lemon
3 tablespoons oil
salt and pepper

4–8 kebab skewers

This is the simplest version of the famous Russian kebab called shashlik. For addi-

tional ingredients for shashlik: add halved lambs kidneys, mushrooms, pieces of onion, or cherry tomatoes to skewers, spices or herbs like coriander and caraway, oregano, thyme and rosemary to marinade.

Method
Combine the ingredients for the marinade, mix in the lamb cubes so they are thoroughly coated, cover and let stand 2–5 hours, stirring the meat occasionally so it is well coated in marinade.

   Thread the meat (with any other ingredients) tightly on skewers. Broil 3–4 inches from heat for 5 minutes on each side if you like the lamb pink; 6–7 minutes for well done lamb. Serve with pilaf (see page 115).

Ukrainian Beet Salad

2 lb cooked beets, peeled
1½ tablespoons grated fresh
   horseradish
2 tablespoons sugar
¼ cup white vinegar
½ teaspoon caraway seeds (or
   to taste)

Serve with pickled herring.

Method
Grate the beets coarsely and mix them with the remaining ingredients. Cover and chill at least 2 hours before serving.

Kulebiaka

3½ cup quantity sour cream
   pastry (see page 113)
bunch of watercress (for
   garnish)

For filling
6 hard-cooked eggs, chopped
2 lb piece of salmon
4 cups court bouillon
3 tablespoons butter
1 large onion, finely chopped
2 cups rice

For duxelles
3 cups (¾ lb) mushrooms, finely
   chopped
3 shallots or 1 medium onion,
   finely chopped
3 tablespoons butter
1 tablespoon chopped parsley
1 teaspoon chopped chives
salt and pepper

Kulebiaka can be prepared up to 12 hours ahead, then baked just before serving.

Method
To make the filling: pour the court bouillon over the salmon in a baking dish, cover with foil and bake in a moderate oven (350°F) for 20 minutes or until the fish flakes easily when tested with a fork. Cool, then strain the liquid and add enough water to make 1 quart; reserve it. Lift the salmon off the bone in as large pieces as possible, discarding the skin and bone. Leave oven on.

   In a flameproof casserole heat 3 tablespoons butter, fry the onion until soft but not brown and stir in the rice. Cook, stirring for 2–3 minutes until the grains look transparent and pour on the reserved cooking liquid from the salmon. Bring to a boil, cover and bake in heated oven for 15 minutes. Add a little more water if the rice looks dry and cook 5–7 minutes

longer until all liquid has been absorbed and the rice is tender. Let stand 10 minutes before removing the cover and stirring the rice.

   To make the duxelles: in a skillet melt the butter and cook the shallot or onion until soft. Add the mushrooms and cook over high heat, stirring occasionally for 3–4 minutes until all the moisture has evaporated. Stir in the herbs and season well.

   Roll out the sour cream pastry dough on a floured board to a 14 X 10 inch rectangle. Arrange chopped hard-cooked egg in a 10 X 3½ inch strip in the middle of the dough. Spread the duxelles mixture on top, then set the pieces of salmon neatly on top of that. Pile the rice mixture on the salmon, molding it with the hands or the back of a spoon so the rectangle of filling is as tall and as neat as possible.

   Cut a square of excess dough from each corner and brush the edges of the dough rectangle with egg glaze. Lift one long edge of the dough on top of the filling and fold over the opposite edge to enclose it. Press gently to seal the dough and fold over the ends to make a neat package. Roll the package over onto a baking sheet so that the joined ends of dough are underneath. Brush the kulebiaka with glaze.

   Roll out the excess dough into a long strip and cut it into narrow bands, preferably with a fluted cutter. Lay the bands over the kulebiaka to decorate it and press 1 long band around the base to finish the edge.

   Turn oven up to hot (400°F). Brush the kulebiaka again with glaze and bake in heated oven for 15 minutes or until the pastry starts to brown. Turn down the heat to moder-

Kulebiaka is served on a platter garnished with watercress. It is cut lengthwise, then sliced and served with melted butter separately

ate (350°F) and bake 30 minutes longer or until a skewer inserted in the center of the kulebiaka for 1 minute is hot to the touch when withdrawn.

To serve: set the kulebiaka on a platter and garnish the dish with watercress. Cut it lengthwise down the center and then crosswise into slices. Serve with melted butter.

On pastry dough arrange duxelles mixture, egg and salmon

Pile rice mixture on salmon to make a tall, neat rectangle

Fold over long edges of pastry dough, then fold over ends

117

Vatrushka
(Cottage Cheese Cake)

For sour cream pastry
2 cups flour
½ teaspoon salt
½ cup butter
½ cup sugar
1 teaspoon vanilla
2 tablespoons sour cream

For cottage cheese filling
1½ cups (¾ lb) dry cottage cheese
6 tablespoons butter, softened
¾ cup confectioners' sugar
grated rind of 1 orange
⅓ cup chopped candied orange peel
½ cup golden raisins
3 tablespoons sour cream

10 inch flan ring, or pie pan with removable base

Method

Make the sour cream pastry dough (see page 113), adding the vanilla with the sour cream. Chill 1 hour.

Set oven at moderately hot (375°F).

Roll out the pastry dough and line it into the flan ring or pie pan. Prick the base, line it with wax or silicone paper, fill with beans or rice and bake blind in heated oven for 20 minutes or until lightly browned, removing the paper and beans after 15 minutes cooking. Let the pastry shell cool.

To make the cottage cheese filling: work the cheese through a sieve and beat in the butter and sugar. Stir in the grated orange rind with candied orange peel, raisins and sour cream. Spread the mixture in the cooked pastry shell, smooth the top, then remove the vatrushka from flan ring or pie pan. Chill the cheesecake thoroughly before serving.

Caucasian Walnut Candy

For 2 lb candy: brown 3 cups finely chopped walnuts in a moderate oven (350°F) for 10–12 minutes.
Watchpoint: do not brown them too much or the candy will be bitter.

In a heavy-based pan, heat ½ cup sugar with 2 cups honey until dissolved, add ½ teaspoon ground cardamom, then bring to a boil and cook steadily until the mixture reaches 220°F on a sugar thermometer.

Take from the heat, stir in the walnuts, then cook gently for 5–7 minutes, stirring constantly, or until the candy draws from the sides of the pan and reaches 280°F on sugar thermometer.

Turn the candy onto an oiled baking sheet and spread out ½ inch thick. Let cool until almost firm, then cut it with a sharp oiled knife into diamonds.

Angelica is a herb valued for its leaves and its root, and it is used in cordials and liqueurs such as Chartreuse. Candied angelica is made from the stalks; it comes in wide, flat strips and is generally cut up to use with other candied fruits for decoration.

Charlotte Russe

1 package lemon gelatine
few candied cherries
candied angelica, cut in small diamond shapes
12 ladyfingers

For Bavarian cream
1¼ cups milk
1 vanilla bean or ½ teaspoon vanilla extract
3 egg yolks
3 tablespoons sugar
1 envelope unflavored gelatin
1 cup heavy cream

Charlotte mold (1 quart capacity)

Method

Prepare the lemon gelatine as directed on the package and, when cool but still liquid, pour enough onto bottom of charlotte mold to measure ¼ inch. Chill until firm.

Arrange a pattern of cherries and angelica diamonds on the layer of gelatine and carefully spoon a little more gelatine on top to set the design. Chill mold; pour the remaining gelatine into a shallow pan to set.

Trim the sides of the ladyfingers neatly and arrange them close together around the sides of the mold.

To make the Bavarian cream: scald the milk with vanilla bean, if using, and leave to infuse 10 minutes (to absorb the flavor). If using vanilla extract, do not add at this point. Beat the egg yolks and sugar together until thick and light. Remove vanilla bean and gradually pour the infused milk over the egg mixture, stirring constantly. Return the mixture to pan and cook the custard over low heat, stirring, until it coats the back of a spoon.

Watchpoint: do not boil or the custard will curdle. Should this happen, quickly pour the mixture into a cold mixing bowl and beat hard with a whisk for 1–2 minutes.

Strain the custard into a bowl. In a pan sprinkle unflavored gelatin over 3 tablespoons cold water and let stand 5 minutes until spongy; set pan in hot water to dissolve gelatin. Stir into custard and let mixture cool. If vanilla extract is used, stir it in now.

Whip cream until it holds a soft shape and refrigerate.

Place the custard in a saucepan over a bowl of cold water to which ice cubes have been added. Chill the mixture, stirring occasionally, until it begins to thicken. Fold in the whipped cream and pour at once into the prepared mold. Cover and refrigerate 3–4 hours or until firm.

To serve: dip the bottom of the mold quickly in and out of hot water and unmold onto a platter (silver is traditional but any decorative one can be used). Turn out remaining gelatin onto a sheet of damp wax paper and chop with a wet knife; arrange around base of the charlotte russe.

Arrange a neat rim of ladyfingers around the charlotte mold before adding the Bavarian cream filling

RUSSIAN EASTER

Easter is still one of the greatest festivals in the Russian calendar. The traditional feast is held at 1 a.m. after church on Saturday night. The meal always includes a roast leg of lamb or veal, or a baked ham, and cucumber and radish salad, herring, and painted hard-cooked eggs.

The eggs can vary from the simple decorated ones that are eaten at the feast to the intricate Ukrainian egg shells patterned with brilliant black, red and green geometric designs that are passed from generation to generation.

Among the traditional foods eaten at Easter are kulich — a rich spiced bread also called baba — and paskha — a sweetened cheese mold shaped in a pyramid — that have been blessed in church and form the centerpiece on the table.

Kulich and Paskha Molds

Molds for kulich and paskha are hard to find here.

Kulich is a rich yeast bread traditionally shaped like a tall, thick-stemmed mushroom — use a tall can (1 quart 14 oz) with the lid cut out, such as a coffee or juice can, for baking it.

Paskha is a rich cheese and sugar mixture that is molded in a pyramid in a metal or wooden mold. If you cannot find one, use a clean porous plant pot of the type with a hole for drainage.

Kulich

1 cup milk
¾ cup sugar
1 package dry or 1 cake compressed yeast
4 cups flour
½ teaspoon salt
3 egg yolks
¾ cup unsalted butter
½ cup chopped mixed candied fruits
½ cup whole blanched almonds, browned and ground
½ cup golden raisins
pinch of saffron, soaked in ¼ cup boiling water for 30 minutes
3 cardamom pods, seeds removed and crushed to a powder
1 teaspoon vanilla
colored sugar (for sprinkling)

For icing
1 cup confectioners' sugar
about 1 tablespoon water

2 empty juice cans (1 quart 14 oz each) lids removed

Makes 2 kulichi.

Method
Line the sides of the cans with wax paper or foil, leaving a 3 inch collar above the top of the can. Fasten the join in the collar securely with a paperclip. Thoroughly grease the base of the cans and the paper or foil.

Scald the milk and cool it to lukewarm. In a bowl mix the lukewarm milk with ½ cup sugar and sprinkle over the yeast. Let stand 5 minutes or until dissolved. Sift ½ cup flour with the salt into a bowl and gradually stir in the yeast mixture to make a smooth batter. Cover the bowl with a cloth and let rise 1 hour or until the batter is full of bubbles.

Beat the egg yolks with the remaining sugar until thick and light and beat this mixture into the yeast batter. Melt the butter and sift the remaining flour.

With the hand beat the flour and butter alternately into the yeast mixture to form a smooth soft dough. Beat in the candied fruits, almonds, golden raisins, strained saffron liquid, cardamom powder and vanilla and continue beating with the hand or the dough hook of an electric mixer for 15–20 minutes or until the dough is very smooth and elastic.

Cover the bowl with a damp cloth and let the dough rise again in a warm place until doubled in bulk. Knead lightly to knock out the air, divide in two and put the dough into the prepared cans to fill them half full. Leave in a warm place to rise until the dough reaches the tops of the cans. Set the oven at moderate (350°F).

When the dough has risen, bake it in heated oven for 1 hour or until the breads sound hollow when tapped. The dough will rise and mushroom over the tops of the cans during baking. Turn the breads out onto a wire rack to cool.

Mix the confectioners' sugar to a smooth soft icing with the water. Stand the breads upright and pour the icing over the tops of the breads so it drips down the sides. Quickly sprinkle the tops with colored sugar. For Easter the bread traditionally is topped with a red paper rose.

To serve: cut the mushroom top from the bread and slice the bread in rounds; use the top as a lid to keep any remaining bread fresh.

Paskha

4 cups cottage cheese
1½ cups sugar
1 cup sour cream
4 egg yolks
1 vanilla bean
¼ cup whole blanched almonds, chopped
½ cup chopped mixed candied fruits

Special metal or wooden paskha mold or plant pot (1½–2 quart capacity); 2 pieces of double cheesecloth

Method
Put the cottage cheese in a piece of cheesecloth and hang it up for 3–4 hours to drain off all moisture. Work the cottage cheese through a very fine strainer. Beat in the sugar and stir in the sour cream, egg yolks and vanilla bean. Transfer the mixture to a large saucepan and heat gently, stirring until the mixture just begins to bubble around the edges.

Watchpoint: do not let the mixture boil.

Cool the mixture, and stir in the almonds and candied fruits. Put it back into the cheesecloth and hang it up to drain for 12 hours.

Line the clean cheesecloth into the paskha mold or plant pot as smoothly as possible and fill with the cheese mixture, packing it down well and removing vanilla bean. Fold over the cheesecloth on top of the mixture and set a flat plate with a 2 lb weight on top. Let stand in a bowl in the refrigerator for 18–24 hours.

To serve, unmold the paskha onto a platter and carefully peel off the cheesecloth. Top the mold with a paper rose — usually no other decoration is added.

Selection of cold meats includes spiced beef (on stand), chicken and ham à l'anglaise (in bowl, left, and turned out on a platter), and poultry in aspic (at front)

COOKING FOR A COLD SUPPER

Cold meats are a splendid standby for the holiday season. They can be prepared well ahead of a special occasion so that you need only a bowl or two of salad and a choice of dessert to complete a tempting menu.

Most cold meats keep well in the refrigerator for 4–5 days so they are an excellent source of snacks and sandwiches and offer an easy solution to the problem of unexpected guests.

Serve the following cold meats with a piquant dressing or a sweet and sour Cumberland sauce, made with red currant jelly and orange juice.

Spiced Beef

5 lb brisket of beef
2 cloves of garlic, slivered

For spice mixture
6 tablespoons dark brown
    sugar
1 oz saltpeter
1 tablespoon allspice berries,
    crushed
2 bay leaves, crushed
$\frac{1}{3}$ cup salt

For cooking
2 onions, quartered
2 carrots, quartered
1 stalk of celery, sliced
large bouquet garni

Piece of cheesecloth

Method
Make small incisions in the
meat with the point of a knife
and insert the garlic slivers
into the incisions.

To make the spice mixture:
mix the sugar, saltpeter, allspice, bay leaves and salt
together thoroughly and rub
well over the meat. Cover and
keep in the refrigerator for
1 week, rubbing the meat
each day with the spice mixture.

Remove the meat, tie it
tightly in cheesecloth to keep
its shape and put in a kettle
with the vegetables and bouquet garni. Cover with cold
water, add the lid and simmer
3–4 hours or until the meat is
tender.

Cool in the liquid until
tepid, take out the meat,
remove the cheesecloth, set
the meat in a deep dish, put a
plate or board on top and
add a 4–6 lb weight. Leave
overnight in the refrigerator.
Remove the weight and serve
the beef plain or brushed with
meat glaze.

Saltpeter can be bought
in a pharmacy, and is
added to many sausages
and salted meats as a pre-
servative; it also gives
meat a clear pink color.

Meat Glaze

True meat glaze is made
by boiling strained brown
bone stock until it is thick
and syrupy and less than
1 cup mixture is left. Cool
the glaze to lukewarm
before brushing or spoon-
ing it over meat to coat it.
(The lesson on stocks in
Volume 2 included a
recipe for brown bone
stock.)
Mock meat glaze can be
made with canned con-
sommé: sprinkle 1 en-
velope gelatin over $\frac{1}{2}$ can
consommé in a small
pan, leave 5 minutes until
spongy, then dissolve
over a pan of hot water.
Stir in remaining con-
sommé and use the glaze
when cool and on point of
setting.

Note: all the cold supper
recipes on pages 122–129
serve 6–8 people.

Boiled Corned Beef

4–5 lb piece of corned beef
    (preferably brisket)
10 peppercorns
large bouquet garni
2 onions, quartered
2 carrots, quartered
1 stalk of celery, cut in quarters

Method
Cut the beef in half and put in
a large kettle with the peppercorns, bouquet garni, vegetables and water to cover.
Add a lid and simmer 3–4
hours or until meat is tender.

While still hot, transfer the
meat to a deep dish and put
one piece of beef on top of
the other. Insert a toothpick or short skewer vertically
through each end, pressing
the skewers down level with
the top of the meat.

Put a board or plate on
top, add a 4–5 lb weight and
refrigerate overnight. Remove
the weight and board and
brush with 2–3 coats of meat
glaze.

Piquant Dressing for Cold Meats

In a screwtop jar combine 6
tablespoons dark brown
sugar, 6 tablespoons wine
vinegar, $\frac{3}{4}$ cup oil, 1 tablespoon prepared mustard, a
little salt and freshly ground
black pepper. Shake vigo-
rously to blend well; taste for
seasoning.

This dressing keeps for up
to 2 weeks in the refrigerator,
but warm it before using to
melt the oil.

Cumberland Sauce

Cut 2–3 strips of rind from an
orange with a vegetable
peeler. Cut into thin strips
and blanch in boiling water
for 1 minute. Drain, refresh
and drain again.

Over gentle heat melt
$\frac{1}{2}$ cup red currant jelly with
the juice of $\frac{1}{2}$ lemon, $\frac{1}{4}$ cup
port and the juice from the
orange. Let cool before adding the orange rind.

Pressed Tongue

1 large or 2 medium fresh or
    smoked beef tongues
    ($4\frac{1}{2}$–6 lb total)
1 large carrot
1 large onion, peeled
6–8 peppercorns
salt
1–2 bay leaves

*Tongue press, springform pan,
or soufflé dish*

Method
Put the tongue in a large
kettle, cover with cold water,
add the lid and bring slowly to
a boil. Add all the other ingredients and simmer 4–5 hours
for a large tongue or 2–3 hours
for medium ones or until very
tender.

A smoked tongue takes
longer to cook than a fresh
one. Test by pulling out a
small bone at the base of the
tongue – if it comes out easily,
the tongue is done. Also stick
the point of a knife into the
thickest part of the tongue –
it will slip in easily when the
meat is tender.
Watchpoint: it is almost impossible to overcook a tongue,
so give it plenty of time to
cook because it is rubbery if
underdone.

Cool the tongue in the
liquid, then drain and put in a
bowl of cold water – this

makes it easy to handle. Peel off the skin, cut away any gristle or membrane and remove any bones. Curl the tongue around and push it into the tongue press, springform pan or soufflé dish (it should fit closely). Put both tongues in the same container if using medium tongues.

Screw the tongue press down as tightly as possible or press down well with a small plate with a weight on top if no press is available. Chill overnight and turn out. Pressed tongue can be stored, covered, in the refrigerator for up to 1 week.

Cut the tongue in thin slices and serve with Cumberland sauce.

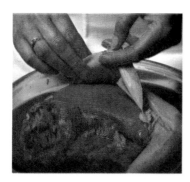

Remove the skin from the tongue after cooling it in the cooking liquid

Curl the tongue around and push it into the tongue press so it fits closely

Screw the tongue press down as tightly as possible

Steak and Squab Tourtière

2 lb lean beef, finely ground
2 squabs
1 small onion, finely chopped
3 tablespoons oil
$2\frac{1}{2}$ cups stock
salt and pepper
$\frac{1}{2}$ cup sherry
bouquet garni
$\frac{1}{2}$ envelope gelatin

For pastry
3 cups flour
1 teaspoon salt
$\frac{2}{3}$ cup butter
$\frac{1}{3}$ cup shortening
1 egg yolk
3–4 tablespoons water
1 egg, beaten to mix with
$\frac{1}{2}$ teaspoon salt (for glaze)

8 inch springform pan

Method
Make the pastry dough and chill 30 minutes.

Set the oven at moderate (350°F).

In a flameproof casserole, cook the onion in 2 tablespoons of the oil until soft. Increase heat, add the beef and fry briskly until browned, stirring constantly. Add $1\frac{1}{2}$–2 cups stock, season, cover pot and cook in heated oven for 1 hour or until the mixture is thick. Cool.

In another flameproof casserole, brown the squabs on all sides in remaining oil, add half the sherry, cover tightly and cook in the oven with the beef for 30 minutes or until the birds are tender. Cool, take the meat from the bones and cut into neat fillets. Return bones to the pot, add bouquet garni, remaining sherry and stock and simmer 30 minutes.

Increase oven temperature to moderately hot (375°F).

Roll out two-thirds of the pastry dough fairly thickly and line the bottom and sides of the springform pan; prick the base. Fill the pastry shell with alternate layers of beef mixture and the squab fillets, starting and ending with beef.

Roll out the remaining dough and cut an 8 inch circle. Moisten the edges of the pastry shell, lift on the circle of dough to form a lid and trim; press the edges firmly to seal.

Roll out the pastry trimmings and cut leaves for decoration. Make a hole in the center of the pie with the point of a knife and arrange the leaves around it. Brush the pie with beaten egg and bake in heated oven for 45–50 minutes or until browned.

Strain the stock from the squab bones (there should be about $\frac{3}{4}$ cup). Sprinkle the gelatin over 2 tablespoons water, let stand 5 minutes until spongy, then stir into the hot stock until dissolved. Pour into the tourtière through the center hole while still warm, then let cool.

A **tourtière**, often called a **tourte**, is a round deep double crust pie, usually filled with a savory rather than a sweet mixture. Tourtière also refers to the traditional round earthenware mold in which a tourte should be cooked.

Poultry in Aspic

2 squabs or rock Cornish game
  hens
2½ lb roasting chicken
4 lb duck
½ lb lean pork, cut in large
  cubes
1 large onion, peeled
1 carrot
large bouquet garni
strip of lemon rind
salt and pepper
¼ lb cooked ham, cut in strips

For stuffing balls
¾ lb loose sausage meat
1 tablespoon chopped parsley
2 tablespoons fresh white
  breadcrumbs
1 egg white, beaten to mix
2–3 cups beef stock (for
  poaching)

For aspic
stock (from cooking poultry)
¼ cup port or sherry per quart
  of stock (optional)
1–1½ envelopes gelatin per
  quart of stock

*2 terrines or deep dishes (2–3
quart capacity each)*

Method
With a damp cloth wipe all the
birds, then put them in a
large kettle. Add the pork,
onion, carrot, bouquet garni,
lemon rind and seasoning and
cover with cold water. Add
pan lid and simmer 1–1½
hours or until the birds and
pork are very tender. Remove
the squabs or Cornish hens
after 30 minutes cooking and
the chicken after 45 minutes
cooking, or as soon as they
are tender.
Watchpoint: to avoid cloud-
ing the aspic, be sure the
poultry simmers but does not
boil during cooking. When
reducing the stock skim it
often.
  To make the stuffing balls:
mix the sausage meat, pars-

ley, breadcrumbs and seasoning. Stir in the egg white to
bind the mixture and roll into
walnut-sized balls.
  Set balls in a large shallow
pan in one layer, pour over the
stock to cover, add the pan lid
and poach for 12–15 minutes.
Cool the balls in the stock,
then drain carefully.
  Lift the pork and duck from
the kettle, remove the bones
and pull all the meat into
strips with 2 forks, discarding
any skin. Strain the stock,
return to the kettle, add ¼ cup
sherry or port for every quart
of stock, if you like, and
reduce by boiling until strong
and well flavored; if necessary, add more seasoning
towards the end of reduction.
Chill until set and remove fat.
  To make aspic: melt the
stock, measure, and for each
quart sprinkle 1–1½ envelopes
gelatin over 1 cup of the stock
in a small pan — more gelatin
is needed for stock that is not
well jelled. Stand 5 minutes
until spongy. Dissolve over a
pan of hot water and stir into
remaining stock.
  Layer the pork and poultry,
ham strips and stuffing balls in
terrines or deep dishes. Carefully pour in just enough of the
cool stock to cover.
  Cover and chill until set —
the aspic will keep, uncut, for
2–3 days in the refrigerator.

Note: all the cold supper
recipes on pages 122–129
serve 6–8 people.

Boeuf à la Mode Bourgeoise

2 lb chuck or round roast of
  beef, cut in 1 inch cubes
2 lb boneless loin of pork,
  cut in 1 inch cubes
1 calf's foot, split
1 pig's foot, split
2 onions, chopped
2 carrots, chopped
3 stalks of celery, chopped
2 cloves of garlic, crushed
5 whole cloves
1 teaspoon ground allspice
12 peppercorns
salt
bouquet garni
1 cup red wine
1–1½ cups stock

*Terrine or deep serving
  bowl (2½–3 quart capacity)*

Method
Blanch the calf's and pig's
feet: put them in a large pan of
cold water, bring it to a boil,
simmer 5 minutes and drain.
Lay them in a large casserole
and put the beef, pork and
vegetables on top in layers,
sprinkling each layer with a
little garlic, cloves, allspice,
peppercorns and salt.
  Add the bouquet garni to
the pot, pour over the wine
and stock, cover and cook
in a moderately low oven
(325°F) for 3–4 hours or until
the calf's and pig's feet are
very tender. If the mixture
gets dry, add more stock —
about 1½ cups liquid should
be left at end of cooking.
  Let the mixture cool slightly,
then lift out the beef and pork
and pull it into shreds with 2
forks, or leave it in cubes, if
you like. Pull the meat from the
calf's and pig's feet into shreds
and put with the pork and beef
in the terrine or bowl.
  Strain the cooking liquid,
pressing the mixture well to
extract all the juice, taste for
seasoning and pour over the

meat. Press down well, cover
and chill until set.
  Serve beef mixture in
terrine or bowl and cut in
slices.

Chicken and Ham à l'Anglaise

3½–4 lb roasting chicken
1 lb cooked lean ham, cut in
  strips
1 calf's foot or 1 lb veal
  bones
2 onions, quartered
2 carrots, quartered
bouquet garni
6 peppercorns
1 cup white wine
juice of ½ lemon
salt and pepper

Bowl (2 quart capacity)

Method
If using a calf's foot, split it
open with a sharp knife, put in
a pan, cover with cold water,
and bring to a boil; simmer 5
minutes and drain.
  In a large kettle put the
chicken with the calf's foot or
veal bones, vegetables, bouquet garni, peppercorns,
white wine and water to
cover. Add lid and simmer
1 hour or until bird is tender.
  Cool until lukewarm in the
liquid, then lift out the chicken
and take the meat from the
bones, cutting it in strips and
discarding skin. Return bones
to liquid in pan; boil stock without lid until reduced to 3 cups.
  Strain the stock, add the
lemon juice with seasoning to
taste and stir in the chicken
and ham. Transfer the mixture
to the bowl, cover and chill
until set. Remove any fat
from the surface and turn out
just before serving.

Galantine of Veal

3–4 lb breast of veal, boned
2 onions, quartered
2 carrots, quartered
large bouquet garni
6 peppercorns
½ teaspoon salt
meat glaze (see page 122)

For stuffing
¾ cup (6 oz) ground cooked ham
½ lb ground pork
1 small onion, finely chopped
2 tablespoons butter
1½ cups fresh white
    breadcrumbs
2 tablespoons shelled
    pistachios, split in two
1 small egg, beaten to mix

Trussing needle and fine string;
scalded dish towel

Method

To make the stuffing: thoroughly mix the ground ham and pork in a bowl. Cook the onion in the butter until soft. Add to the meat with the breadcrumbs and nuts and season well. Stir in beaten egg to bind the mixture.

Spread the stuffing on the inside surface of the veal, tuck in the ends and roll to an even cylinder. Sew or tie with string. Wrap tightly in a scalded dish towel so the galantine keeps its shape. Tie at each end and fasten the cloth in the center with a safety pin.

Immerse the galantine in a kettle of boiling water with vegetables and seasonings. Cover and simmer 1½ hours.

Take out the galantine, cool a little, unwrap the cloth and reroll it around the meat as tightly as possible. Put in a deep dish, rest a board or plate on top and add a 2 lb weight to press the meat lightly. Chill overnight; remove the board, weight and cloth and brush with meat glaze.

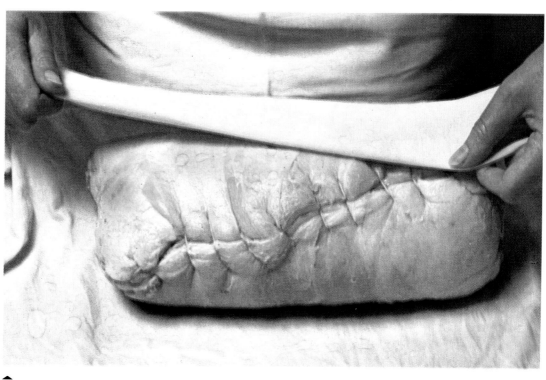

Wrap the sewn-up boned, stuffed veal in a dish towel

Fasten the dish towel securely around the galantine

Pineapple charlotte adds eye appeal to a buffet table

DESSERTS

No buffet, however simple, is complete without an eye-catching dessert. If you like, prepare these recipes in advance and unmold, if necessary, and decorate them just before serving.

Pineapple Charlotte

1 can (14 oz) pineapple slices
2½ cups milk
4 egg yolks
3 tablespoons sugar
1 teaspoon arrowroot
1 envelope gelatin
2 egg whites
1½ cups heavy cream, whipped until it holds a stiff peak
1 package cats' tongues cookies or ladyfingers

7 inch springform pan or charlotte mold (1½ quart capacity); pastry bag and a star tube

Method
Scald the milk. Beat the egg yolks with the sugar and arrowroot until the mixture is thick and light. Stir in the hot milk, return the mixture to the pan and cook, stirring, until the custard thickens; do not let it boil. Strain and cool.

Drain the pineapple, reserving the juice and 5 slices for decoration, and chop remaining slices. Sprinkle the gelatin over ¼ cup of pineapple juice in a small pan and let stand 5 minutes until spongy. Dissolve over a pan of hot water, stir into the custard and let cool.

Beat the egg whites until they hold a stiff peak. Set the custard over a pan of ice water and chill until on the

point of setting. Fold two-thirds of the whipped cream into the custard mixture, then fold in the egg whites and the chopped pineapple. Pour the mixture into the pan or mold and chill 2 hours or until set.

Just before serving, loosen the mold around the edges and turn out onto a platter. Spread the sides with some of the remaining whipped cream and arrange the cookies or ladyfingers around the sides of the mold, overlapping them slightly.

Decorate the top of the charlotte with the remaining pineapple slices and the remaining whipped cream, piped in rosettes, using a pastry bag fitted with the star tube.

Port Wine Gelatin

1 bottle port
1 inch piece of cinnamon stick
3 strips of lemon rind
¾ cup sugar
3 envelopes gelatin
2 cups water

Decorative gelatin mold (1½ quart capacity)

Method
Pour half the port into a saucepan (not aluminum), bring to a boil, simmer 2–3 minutes and add the cinnamon, lemon rind and sugar. Cover and leave to infuse for 10 minutes.

Sprinkle gelatin over water and let stand 5 minutes. Add to the pan containing the infused port, heat gently until gelatin is dissolved and add remaining port. Rinse the mold with cold water, strain gelatin into it and chill 2–3 hours or until set. Just before serving, dip mold into warm water and turn onto a platter.

Key Lime Pie

1½ cup quantity of rich pie pastry (see Volume 1)

For filling
¾ cup fresh lime juice
3 egg yolks
14 oz can condensed milk

For meringue
3 egg whites
½ cup sugar

9 inch pie pan

Method
Make the pie pastry dough and chill. Line the pie pan and bake blind.

To make the filling: beat the egg yolks and condensed milk thoroughly and stir in the lime juice. Pour the filling into the pie shell.

To make the meringue: beat the egg whites until they hold a stiff peak. Beat in 2 tablespoons sugar until glossy and fold in the remaining sugar with a metal spoon.

Pile the meringue on the filling, sealing it to the pastry to avoid shrinkage. Bake in a low oven (275°F) for 15 minutes or until the meringue is lightly browned. Let cool.

Alternative Topping
If you prefer, the pie can be covered with cream instead of meringue. Stiffly whip 1 cup heavy cream, fill into a pastry bag fitted with a star tube and pipe the cream in small rosettes to cover the pie completely. Sprinkle the top with 2 teaspoons grated lime rind.

Pears in Red Currant Jelly

6–8 firm, ripe pears
1½ cups red currant jelly
¾ cup sugar
1¾ cups water
pared rind and juice of 1½ lemons

For serving
¾ cup heavy cream, whipped until it holds a stiff shape
3 tablespoons brandy or 1½ teaspoons vanilla
2 tablespoons sugar

Method
To make the syrup: dissolve the sugar in the water, bring slowly to a boil, add the lemon juice and rind and simmer 5 minutes.

Keep the stems on the pears; pare them and remove the 'eye' from the bases. Place the pears in the prepared syrup, cover and poach them until tender. Even when the pears are ripe, this must take 20–30 minutes to prevent discoloration around the cores.

Drain the pears and arrange them in a serving bowl. Boil the syrup until reduced to 1 cup. Add the red currant jelly, heat gently until dissolved and simmer the mixture until it is the consistency of maple syrup. Let cool to tepid, then spoon over the pears. Chill thoroughly.

Beat the brandy or vanilla and sugar into the whipped cream until the cream thickens again and serve separately.

Note: all the cold supper recipes on pages 122–129 serve 6–8 people.

Nesselrode Pudding

2 cans chestnut purée
  (15½ oz each)
½ cup raisins
½ cup golden raisins
½ cup candied cherries,
  chopped
½ cup candied orange
  rind, chopped
¼ cup maraschino liqueur
1 cup heavy cream, whipped
  until it holds a soft shape

For custard
2 cups light cream
1 vanilla bean, split or
  1 teaspoon vanilla extract
¾ cup sugar
4 egg yolks

For decoration
8–10 glacé chestnuts
½ cup heavy cream, stiffly
  whipped

*Bombe mold (6–8 cup capacity)
  – optional; pastry bag and
  medium star tube*

If no bombe mold is available,
a rounded metal bowl (1½–2
quart capacity) is a good
substitute.

Method

Pour over boiling water to
cover both kinds of raisins, let
stand 15 minutes until they
are plump and drain them.
Add the candied cherries and
orange rind, pour over the
maraschino liqueur, cover
and let macerate.

To make the custard: if
using vanilla bean, infuse it
in the light cream for 10 minutes, keeping the pan covered;
take the bean and stir in the
sugar. Do not add vanilla
extract at this point.

Beat the egg yolks in a bowl
until they are light colored,
scald the sugar and cream
mixture and gradually stir
into the yolks. Return the

mixture to the pan and stir
over low heat until the custard
thickens enough to coat the
back of a spoon.

Watchpoint: do not let the
custard boil.

Add vanilla extract if using.
Strain the custard, sprinkle it
with sugar to prevent a skin
from forming and let cool.

Stir in the chestnut purée
with the macerated fruits and
maraschino liqueur into the
cool custard. Fold in the
lightly whipped cream. Pour
the mixture into the mold or
bowl, cover tightly and freeze
3–4 hours or until the pudding is firmly set. It can be
stored in the freezer for up to
2 months.

To serve: if preparing in
advance, transfer bombe or
bowl to refrigerator 4–6
hours before serving for the
mixture to soften to the right
consistency.

Dip the mold or bowl in cold
water and unmold onto a
platter. Decorate the base
with glacé chestnuts and,
using a pastry bag fitted with a
star tube, pipe around rosettes
of whipped cream.

Nesselrode pudding is
named for Count Nessel-
rode, a famous statesman
who directed Russian
foreign policy during the
war with Napoleon.

Glacé chestnuts are whole
chestnuts that have been
simmered in sugar syrup
until they have become
candied. They are a French
delicacy and are available
at specialty food stores.

Porcupine Tipsy Cake

1 cup sweet white wine
¼ cup sherry
¼ cup orange juice
½ cup apricot jam glaze
  (see Volume 1)
½ cup slivered almonds,
  browned

For cake
½ cup flour
½ cup potato starch or
  arrowroot
pinch of salt
5 eggs (2 separated)
1¼ cups sugar
grated rind of 1 lemon

For syllabub
2 large oranges
1 lemon
4–6 tablespoons sugar
1½ cups heavy cream

*Melon mold (2–2½ quart
  capacity)*

Start making this cake 2 days
ahead of time unless you
already have some dry cake.

Method

Grease the mold; sprinkle it
with sugar and flour, discarding the excess. Set oven at
moderate (350°F).

Sift the flour with the potato
starch or arrowroot and salt.

In a bowl beat 3 whole
eggs, 2 egg yolks and sugar
over a pan of hot but not boiling water until the mixture is
thick and leaves a ribbon trail
when beater is lifted. Continue
beating until cool. If using an
electric beater, no heat is
needed.

Beat the remaining egg
whites until they hold a soft
shape. Fold into the egg and
sugar mixture alternately with
the sifted flour mixture and
grated lemon rind, using a
metal spoon.

Pour the mixture into the

prepared mold and bake in
heated oven for 45–60 minutes or until the cake pulls
away from the sides of the
pan. Turn out onto a wire
rack to cool. Leave the cake
overnight because it should
be dry.

Hollow out the top of the
cake with a knife, reserving
the cut-out section. Mix the
wines and orange juice and
pour into the cavity. As the
liquid runs through, baste the
cake so that it is well soaked.
Replace the cake section and
baste again. Cover and leave
overnight.

Melt the apricot jam glaze
and brush over the cake.
Stick the almonds in the top
and sides of the cake to
resemble porcupine quills.

To make the syllabub:
squeeze the oranges and
lemon and measure the juice
– there should be 4 times as
much orange as lemon juice.
Dissolve the sugar in the
fruit juices over low heat;
let cool. Just before serving,
beat the cream until it starts
to thicken, pour in the fruit
juice mixture and continue to
beat until thick. Spoon the
syllabub around the cake.

Syllabub is a traditional
English dessert made by
beating cream with wine
or fruit juice until thick.

Note: all the cold supper
recipes on pages 122–129
serve 6–8 people.

Porcupine tipsy cake is speared with slivered almonds; orange syllabub is spooned around before serving

KINDS OF FATS

Fats are concentrated sources of energy and form a part of all body tissues; they are essential in all normal diets. Little is known about man's fat requirement except that some is needed daily. Even modern food chemists cannot recommend the specific amounts needed in the daily diet.

Fats are oily or greasy substances found in olives, the seeds of some plants, milk, nuts and in animal cells. Fats of animal derivation include butter, bacon fat, lard, suet and chicken fat. Vegetable fats usually come in the form of oil — peanut, olive, safflower, corn, soybean and sesame. Shortening sold in cans is most often made of vegetable oils. Margarine can be all vegetable or made from part animal and part vegetable fats.

In cooking, fats and oils have a variety of uses. Besides adding nutritive value, they give flavor, variety and richness to many dishes. They are used to sauté, shallow or deep fry; they are essential in cakes, pastries and cookies, and they are added to sauces and salad dressings.

Butter

Butter is made from milk and cream that have been churned together until solid. The unsalted kind (often called sweet butter) contains no salt; it does not keep as well as salted butter but recipes call for it when salted butter would give a strong, harsh flavor — particularly in delicate sweet cakes, pastries and frostings.

All butters can be frozen successfully when properly wrapped.

Whipped butter has been whipped together with some inert gas. This increases the volume and makes the butter easy to spread.

The U.S. Government grades the texture, body, color and flavor of butter by score: AA or 93 score, A or 92 score, B or 90 score, C or 89 score.

When butter is used alone for sautéing it scorches easily at a high temperature — the addition of oil retards the scorching. A good ratio is 2 tablespoons butter to 1 tablespoon oil. A butter and oil mixture has reached the proper heat for frying when it foams (showing the water content is evaporating) and the foam dies away. Add the food at this point.

Clarified butter, skimmed of milk solids, is frequently called for in recipes and does not scorch as quickly as ordinary butter. See glossary in Volume 1, or Volume 3.

Margarine or Oleomargarine

This is a fat that resembles butter, and was first made in France in 1870 when Napoleon III offered a prize for a good butter substitute. Within the past decade there has been a constant increase in the use of margarine, mainly because its flavor has been greatly improved. It is available in a solid form or whipped; it, too, can be frozen if properly wrapped.

Margarine can be used as a butter substitute in cooking and in some baking. However, all cakes and cookies that depend on butter for their characteristic flavor and texture are best made with butter.

Lard

A fat rendered from the fatty tissues of pork, lard is used for frying and as a fat in pastry. Until recently it was not popular because of its lack of uniformity of odor, flavor and texture. Within the past few

years, the quality of lard has improved noticeably.

Shortening

Made from vegetable fats or a mixture of vegetable and animal fats, shortening does not need refrigeration and has little or no flavor. It is used in both shallow and deep fat frying, in pastry-making and some cake-making.

Chicken Fat

This fat, used by many good cooks and especially in Jewish cooking, is made by dicing the fat from a chicken, then rendering it in a heavy saucepan over a low heat. Chicken fat keeps almost indefinitely when strained into sterile jars and refrigerated. It is also available rendered in jars in some butcher shops or specialty stores.

Cooking and Salad Oils

Both these are edible oils of vegetable origin. One of the most frequently used is olive oil, with Spanish, French and Italian varieties the most common. All 3 varieties have individual qualities and are used widely in salad dressings, in sautéing and in general cooking, but low quality olive oil is too heavy.

Other excellent oils are made from peanuts, corn, cotton seeds, sesame seeds, poppy seeds, soybeans, safflowers and walnuts. Walnut oil, imported from France, is available in specialty stores.

It is not necessary to refrigerate these vegetable oils; frequently they solidify or turn cloudy if kept in too cold a place. However, they return to their natural state when brought to room temperature.

Points to remember

1 When deep fat has been used at the right temperature so the food added is sealed at once, the fat should acquire little or no taste or odor from the food and can be used again if it is not discolored.

To store fat correctly after deep frying: cool, then strain into a clean container and refrigerate. It can be clarified to a certain extent by dropping a few slices of potato into the fat before it is reheated gently. Then it should be strained and stored until needed.

2 The easiest way to measure solid fat is by displacement. For one-third cup fat, fill a measuring cup two-thirds full of water; add fat a little at a time until the water reaches the 1 cup line. Drain away water; the fat remaining equals one-third of a cup.

Butter and margarine usually come in measured sticks—1 stick equals $\frac{1}{2}$ cup.

3 To test the correct tempera-

ture of deep fat with a thermometer, drop a 1 inch cube of dry bread into the hot fat. When the bread turns golden brown in 1 minute, the temperature is about 360°F; if the cube turns brown in 20 seconds, the temperature is about 375°F; if it browns in less than 20 seconds, the temperature is about 385°F and it should not be heated above this. However, if you often deep fry foods, it is advisable to use a deep fat thermometer.

4 When a recipe says to cream the butter, remove the butter from the refrigerator and let stand at room temperature while you assemble the other ingredients. If you forget, pour boiling water into a bowl, let stand until the bowl is heated, then pour out the water and dry the bowl. Invert the hot bowl over the dish holding the butter.

5 To store fats in a freezer, wrap in airtight packages or store in airtight containers.

MEASURING & MEASUREMENTS

The recipe quantities in the Course are measured in standard level teaspoons, tablespoons and cups and their equivalents are shown below. Any liquid pints and quarts also refer to U.S. standard measures.

When measuring dry ingredients, fill the cup or spoon to overflowing without packing down and level the top with a knife. All the dry ingredients, including flour, should be measured before sifting, although sifting may be called for·later in the instructions.

Butter and margarine usually come in measured sticks (1 stick equals $\frac{1}{2}$ cup) and other bulk fats can be measured by displacement. For $\frac{1}{3}$ cup fat, fill the measuring cup $\frac{2}{3}$ full of water. Add fat until the water reaches the 1 cup mark. Drain the cup of water and the fat remaining equals $\frac{1}{3}$ cup.

For liquids, fill the measure to the brim, or to the calibration line.

Often quantities of seasonings cannot be stated exactly, for ingredients vary in the amount they require. The instructions 'add to taste' are literal, for it is impossible to achieve just the right balance of flavors in many dishes without tasting them.

Liquid measure	Volume equivalent
3 teaspoons	1 tablespoon
2 tablespoons	1 fluid oz
4 tablespoons	$\frac{1}{4}$ cup
16 tablespoons	1 cup or 8 fluid oz
2 cups	1 pint
2 pints	1 quart
4 quarts	1 gallon

OVEN TEMPERATURES

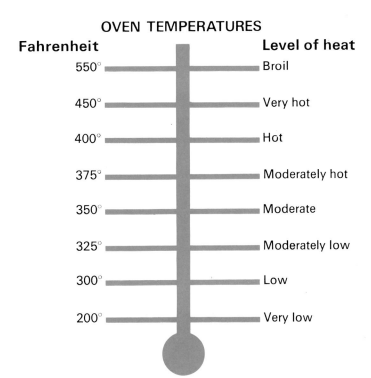

Fahrenheit		Level of heat
550°		Broil
450°		Very hot
400°		Hot
375°		Moderately hot
350°		Moderate
325°		Moderately low
300°		Low
200°		Very low

OVEN TEMPERATURES AND SHELF POSITIONS

Throughout the Cooking Course, oven temperatures are stated in degrees Fahrenheit and in generally agreed levels of heat such as 'high' and 'moderate'. The equivalents are shown on the table above.

However, exact temperature varies in different parts of an oven and the thermostat reading refers to the heat in the middle. As the oven temperature at top and bottom can vary as much as 25°F from this setting, the positioning of shelves is very important. In general, heat rises, so the hottest part of the oven is at the top, but consult the manufacturer's handbook about your individual model.

Pans and dishes of food should be placed parallel with burners or elements to avoid scorched edges.

When baking cakes, there must be room for the heat to circulate in the oven around baking sheets and cake pans; otherwise the underside of the cakes will burn. If baking more than one cake in an oven that has back burners or elements, arrange the cakes side by side. If the oven has side burners, arrange cakes back and front.

Oven thermostats are often inaccurate and are unreliable at extremely high or low temperatures. If you do a great deal of baking or question the accuracy of your oven, use a separate oven thermometer as a check on the thermostat.

Cooking Curiosities

To put it in simple terms, you can either preserve food by delaying decomposition and transforming the flavor (as with smoked salmon), or enclose it in airtight containers (cans, bottles, certain solutions), so most of the original flavor is retained.

Drying was the way of preserving food in prehistoric times; today fruits like apricots and plums are still dried in the sun, while Swiss delicacies of dried beef and ham are produced by hanging in the mountain air.

With the discovery of the uses of fire, man first tasted the delights of smoked meats. Curing meat has been practised for centuries either by drying, smoking or chilling (nowadays refrigerating).

With canning, we come much nearer to modern times. Preserving by canning was invented by a Frenchman in the late 18th century; this process quickly brought fresh food to a very high temperature (to stop the action of bacteria) before hermetically sealing it, and it quickly spread to Britain and the USA.

John Steinbeck paints another side of the preserving picture in his famous book *The Grapes of Wrath* when he tells how the Joads, a family of Oklahoma farmers, prepared for their journey west to California, during a depression summer nearly 40 years ago. The men cut up their two pigs into blocks for salting. Ma Joad then took over and rubbed the meat in coarse salt, laid it block by block in kegs, pounded salt in the spaces, covered each layer with salt and left them to chill overnight. It was on that pork — preserved by a very simple method — that they survived their long, hot summer.

Mrs. Beeton's Household Management (1899), courtesy of Ward, Lock & Co.

INDEX
(Volume 7)

Index

Acknowledgments
Photographs by Fred J. Maroon on pages 44, 51, 52, 72, 73, 82, 83, 110, 112, 114, 115 and 117. Other photographs by Michael Leale, John Ledger, Roger Phillips, John Cowderoy and Gina Harris. Meat information courtesy of Department of Agriculture, Consumer and Marketing Service, Washington D.C. and National Live Stock and Meat Board, Chicago, Illinois.

141

NOTES